Speaking Volumes

Speaking Volumes

How to Get Students Discussing Books—
And Much More

Barry Gilmore

HEINEMANN
Portsmouth, NH

Heinemann
A division of Reed Elsevier Inc.
361 Hanover Street
Portsmouth, NH 03801–3912
www.heinemann.com

Offices and agents throughout the world

The author and publisher wish to thank those who have generously
given permission to reprint borrowed material:

"The Electronic Conversation" by Barry Gilmore was originally
published in *Tennessee English Journal*, Volume 14, October 2003.
Reprinted by permission of the *Tennessee English Journal*.

Library of Congress Cataloging-in-Publication Data
Gilmore, Barry.
    Speaking volumes : how to get students discussing books—and
much more / Barry Gilmore.
      p. cm.
    Includes bibliographical references.
    ISBN 0-325-00915-5 (alk. paper)
  1. English language—Study and teaching (Middle school)—United
States. 2. English language—Study and teaching (Secondary)—
United States. 3. Discussion. 4. Language arts (Middle school)—
United States. 5. Language arts (Secondary)—United States. I. Title.
    LB1631.G47 2006
    428'.0071'273—dc22   2005028371

Editor: Lisa Luedeke
Production editor: Sonja S. Chapman
Cover design: Night & Day Design
Cover photography: Molly Cook
Compositor: Valerie Levy/Drawing Board Studios
Manufacturing: Louise Richardson

Printed in the United States of America on acid-free paper
10 09 08 07 06 RRD   2 3 4 5

1920

Contents

Foreword

Your students love to talk, right? You hear them every day in the parking lot, around their lockers, and in the halls between classes. They talk eagerly, constantly, loudly, conspiratorially: howling, whispering, laughing, interrupting each other, touching, high-fiving. Sometimes, when students are supposed to be quietly seated in their next class, you have to step into the halls and tell the stragglers to quiet down. And in the lunchroom? The din is so deafening that when the cafeteria lady shouts the daily specials, you can't understand a word. Yeah, those kids can talk alright.

But then they come in your classroom and the talk stops. You sit at the front of the class and stare out into the void, "Who'd like to start our discussion on the color symbolism in *The Scarlet Letter?*" you ask.

And suddenly you are looking at an oil painting of thirty teenagers: mute, frozen, unreachable. The sweat starts. In desperation, you begin calling on a few reliable students, the teacher-pleasers, your very own "first responders." If you are lucky, maybe three of them will join you in a game of "gentle inquisition" for a while. So the four of you conduct a conversational charade while twenty-seven other young adults mimic sentient life forms, hearing, understanding, and remembering nothing.

You're about to meet a teacher who, like every one of us, has fallen into that trap. But Barry Gilmore has found not one, but dozens of ways out. Talk about "been there done that!" Barry has developed an array of brilliantly simple ways to get a classroom full of kids talking productively, cogently, and enthusiastically about literature.

This book reminds me that in recent years, so many of us have focused on helping students work in small, peer-led groups called literature circles, book clubs, or peer editing teams. And we've come a long way in developing procedures that make these collaborative structures more effective. But we have neglected the complementary—and certainly more widely used—structure called "whole class discussion." Indeed, large-group discussion is a staple of classroom interaction in English; for many teachers, it is the baseline instructional mode. It's actually pretty stunning to see how slight the literature is on this most routine practice. We do whole class discussion so much, but we need to learn how to do it much better. And Gilmore's here to help show us *how*.

That's the big question this book answers: If I want to lead twenty-five or thirty kids in productive, engaging, sustained conversations about language, literature, and controversial issues how do I do it? Like, tomorrow? How do I shape things like:

the classroom climate

the questions I pose

my own job(s) as the teacher

the use of writing to drive conversation

the range of roles for the kids

the physical classroom setup

the conversational structures

the engagement level?

This sounds like a lot to consider, but Barry begins with small, powerful steps. Once you have tried his simple and accessible strategies like "Lines," "Get Off the Fence," and "The Grid," you'll be off and running. Instead of sitting numbly in their seats, kids will be up and about, thinking, writing, talking and physically manifesting their thinking. There's no hiding or pretending in these kinds of discussions. Then, with the confidence these early successes bring, you'll learn how to bring new life to debates, parliamentary hearings, and other traditional discussion formats. You'll even get help using technology to foster meaningful dialogue among students.

A lot of professional books for teachers claim to be practical; this one really delivers. And for what it is worth, here's a personal guarantee. I have tried almost every strategy in this book with real students in Chicago. They work. Thanks, Barry.

—Smokey Daniels, September 2005

Acknowledgments

Every good teacher knows the best way to come up with the kind of lesson that students will remember for a lifetime: copy it from a better teacher and adapt it to make it your own. I've had the good fortune to be surrounded by better teachers throughout my career; though any faults with the exercises in this book are of my own making, those outstanding colleagues deserve recognition for the excellent ideas at the core of many of these teaching activities.

To begin with, the finest discussion leaders I know are the Issues teachers from the Tennessee Governor's School for International Studies—Paul Fleming, Blanche Deaderick, Ruth Dunning, and my mother, Dr. Sue Gilmore (to whom I'm also indebted for reading every word of my rough drafts). Watching them teach, I often feel like a student myself. I'm equally grateful to my friends and colleagues of the Lausanne Collegiate School Department of English, who discuss literature, teaching strategies, or just about anything else with me as often as I ask; one could not ask for better mentors and compatriots than Brenda Robinette, Ginger Reese, and Alex Kaplan. My thanks are also due to those other teachers I've met and learned from along the way—Patrick Fonzo, Michele Phillips of Facing History and Ourselves, and my own high school English teachers, Bill Brown and Alan Kaplan—all of whom first demonstrated activities that are mentioned or incorporated here. And, like all teachers, I couldn't write such acknowledgments without expressing appreciation for the many students who have taught me to be a better teacher. In particular, for this book, I owe my appreciation to my former student Nadia Gaber.

To Lisa Luedeke and all those at Heinemann who helped make this book a reality, you have both my gratitude and my praise.

Finally, I thank those who make writing and teaching worthwhile—my wife Susanna and my daughters, Katy and Zoe. How anyone could complete a manuscript without such inspiration, distraction, and entertainment as they provide I can't imagine.

Introduction

If your whole picture of how discussions in high school classrooms take place were based on television and the movies, you'd be carrying around a lot of misconceptions. Teachers, you'd think, can spark passionate debate with a single question; they always know the appropriate and funny rejoinder to any point a student makes; they drop bombshell questions—or, better, answers—just at the moment the bell rings.

Those who teach know better. We've stood before classes of disinterested students who haven't done the assigned reading, asked a question we thought would provoke stimulating and lengthy argument, and waited in dismay for even a single response, thinking to ourselves, "Oh great. *Now* what?"

Good classroom discussions do emerge, from time to time, spontaneously. What's more, we get better, with experience, at handling and directing these discussions; like so many aspects of teaching, leading a discussion is a skill that improves with practice. But as a classroom teacher I learned long ago that not every issue I think is worthy of animated discussion will automatically enthuse students, just as I learned that I don't always have the perfect responses to student questions or the perfect plan for keeping discussions under control and making them as productive as possible. I've had my share of train wrecks in the classroom.

The exercises in this book are designed not just to help avoid those wrecks but to improve even those discussions that might flow spontaneously and naturally on a good day or in a good class. They're also designed to make English classes fun and relevant for any group of students, to meet the challenge of connecting even reluctant students to great stories and texts that they might otherwise resist.

These activities can't, of course, turn us into the smooth, insightful teachers of the television classroom—at least, they haven't done it for me. I still have days when I espouse what I believe to be a profound

insight and then wait, frozen, for the bell to ring, only to be disap-
pointed at the mistiming of my dramatic effects while the students
look at me as if I'm daft. I still find myself lobbing questions that land
on the room like a wet tennis ball and realizing that my lesson plan
has just been shot.

More often, though, I remind myself that discussion doesn't stem
from my efforts to be a charismatic teacher but from regular classes of
students sharing and hearing each other's ideas. When I remember to
take myself out of the equation and offer the students frameworks in
which they can freely and safely discuss their own opinions, I'm more
likely to end the class not with some insight of my own but by listening
to the insights of students, or by answering one of the questions I love
most: "Can we finish this activity tomorrow?"

This book is designed to be helpful. It's designed to move teachers
from talking themselves in circles to watching circles of students talking.
It's designed to help you hear the voices of your students—for them to
hear their own voices, in fact. It's also designed to offer activities that
you can easily adapt to your own classroom, your own works, and your
own methods.

My hope is that if you try these methods, *you* will have fun in class,
too—that you'll find yourself not waiting for the bell to ring to punctu-
ate your thoughts but rather surprised when it does.

1 *Before You Begin: Goals and Strategies*

Of course, you will have specific goals and strategies for your own classroom based on the kinds of students you teach, your curriculum, and a host of other factors. Still, I believe that all discussions in English classrooms should aim at reaching some general objectives; good discussion activities should:

- get as many students involved in the process as possible
- raise the overall level of critical thinking about a text or topic in the classroom
- leave students feeling as though they have discovered ideas and achieved tangible results
- prompt students to make personal connections to a text and to language
- emphasize that multiple interpretations of a text can coexist
- enhance and support other kinds of instruction and learning

I think most teachers would agree about the value of reaching such goals. Yet most teachers would also recognize the difficulties presented by reluctant classes or students and difficult teaching situations. The question for many teachers is not "Do I want to reach these goals?" but rather, "*How* do I reach these goals?"

That's why this book exists.

Why These Discussion Techniques?

Regular classroom discussion, in which the teacher simply leads discussion by asking questions and monitoring answers, can certainly meet all of the goals listed above. However, the discussion techniques included here facilitate meeting these goals because they:

- *Keep students moving.* This helps students who are easily distracted or bored, and often makes the classroom a little less structured and less threatening.

- *Keep talkative students from dominating the conversation.* These methods allow the teacher to see which students think in various ways and so elicit a variety of points of view. They also offer ways to keep individual students from speaking too often.

- *Encourage quieter students to take a stand.* Many students who are reluctant to speak in regular classroom settings become more comfortable when they have moved into a space that declares their position for them, or when they know they can speak on equal footing with others.

- *Offer the teacher a way to structure follow-up questions and follow-up activities carefully.* Because the physical format of these discussions is more structured, it is easier to make a point of moving from one topic to another.

- *Allow the discussion to move from the general to the specific or vice versa.* These techniques offer an easy way for the teacher to direct discussion from larger themes toward specific examples or from specific scenes in a text toward larger themes using a clear step-by-step process.

- *Raise the overall level of enthusiasm of the class for engaging in discussion about a work or issue.* These activities encourage discussion, but they can also encourage students to read and think carefully about what they read by raising the interest level of an entire class.

- *Help students and teachers attain important goals: intellectual stimulation, personal involvement with literature and current events, and improved comprehension.* It's important to remember that many state and national standards emphasize not just technical proficiency with language but the connection students make to literature through varied approaches to texts and analysis. The idea here is that these are the skills that will carry students not just through a few years of high-stakes testing and the college environment (which they will) but also through life as literate and thoughtful individuals. (For more information on meeting standards, see the section in the appendix of this book called "A Note About Standards.")

Tips for Preparing Discussions

In the next two sections, I offer some reminders about preparing and leading discussions. You can't be expected to memorize these lists and recall every item on them as you teach—who would want to? Rather,

I suggest returning to the lists from time to time as a refresher and to spark some new ideas about how you frame discussions with your classes. With that in mind, here are some tips for preparation:

- Prepare lists of questions or statements in advance and know the sequence of questions you want to ask.

- Always prepare more questions/statements than you expect to use in a class session.

- Think about the wording of statements. Often, an extreme viewpoint will raise more discussion than a moderate viewpoint. You may sometimes wish to word questions and statements in extreme ways intentionally so as to challenge students' thinking.

- Think about lead-in and follow-up assignments. Written response (both formal and informal), research of factual information, and rereading often work as homework assignments.

- Be prepared to handle a situation in which students have not done the reading. Think about focusing discussion on a single passage or scene; you might even have photocopies of that passage ready for rereading at the start of class.

- Think about your role as a facilitator. What can you do to help structure a free discussion? Is there a list you can make on the board, for instance, as students raise ideas?

- Explain discussion methods one step at a time; for instance, if you've planned three stages or methods of discussion, give directions for each one only as you come to it, not all at once.

Tips for Leading Discussions

- Give students adequate time to respond. Some studies conclude that teachers wait an average of less than one second for students to formulate a response, while students often need up to ten seconds to figure out how to say what they want to say.

- Try to call on as many students as possible. Sometimes, this means saying, "I want the next response to come from someone who has not yet spoken."

- Don't stop a discussion too soon, but don't let it peter out. Stop your class while the discussion is still cooking, then summarize ideas.

- Show respect for all comments and viewpoints, even while you are disagreeing or providing an alternate view.

- Don't answer the questions yourself. Allow your students to come up with the answers and with responses to one another, even if the process feels frustratingly slow.
- Ask questions with multiple answers or provide statements that suggest multiple points of view.
- Organize, summarize, synthesize. Your job is not to force ideas on students but to compile comments and questions into a logical format.
- Set goals. Even if you don't share these with the class, know where you want the discussion to head.
- If you call on students, consider allowing them to "pass" on one question as long as they answer another question soon thereafter (the danger of this method, of course, is that students begin to anticipate and duck the tough questions; I don't use this method all of the time for just this reason).
- Move around physically as you lead a discussion—change the focus and line of sight for students often.
- Avoid rephrasing student responses yourself. Try to get them to rephrase themselves, and use their exact words when you can.
- Be aware that some discussion can heat up to the point where students get upset. If this happens, back off or change the focus of the discussion in some way.
- Create follow-up activities to help students respond after they've had time to think.
- Use the blackboard often. Write down student thoughts and responses. Try making lists of conflicting ideas, or try writing down all ideas and then having students sort them into lists.
- Don't be afraid to admit that you're wrong or don't know an answer.
- Be enthusiastic. The students will follow your lead.

How the Rest of This Book Is Organized

The discussion activities in this book are organized by type. First, you'll find two chapters that focus on the setup of the activity: lines, in which students compare ideas by degrees, and circles, in which students share and interact as a group or class. Next are two chapters that concentrate on the media used to promote classroom discussion. The first, "Big Paper," suggests ways to use poster-sized paper to get students thinking and communicating, while the next chapter, "Technology," offers some approaches for using email, online resources, and word-processing programs to promote student interaction. Finally, after a brief chapter on formal debate methods, you'll find a compendium of discussion ideas based on specific texts that you can use with the lessons presented in this book, as well as a list that summarizes all of the follow-up ideas included in the book.

Within each chapter, a number of specific methods are outlined. In each case, the format of presentation for these methods is the same: a brief introduction, followed by some suggested guidelines for how to use the activity and some ideas about following up the exercise (in some cases, I've also included notes about making your own version of the exercise). In addition, sample handouts or illustrations of the methods accompany each idea. The final section of each method suggests uses of the activity for connecting classes to current issues and events. This section offers ideas for teachers of literature and also those who teach other disciplines—history, global studies, or any other course that grapples with issues that affect the social and political aspects of the world.

By using lists and bullet points as much as possible, I've tried to keep the format of these methods practical and immediately useful. I've also included samples from commonly taught novels and plays for you to use in your class, but you should also view them as models for exercises that you can generate based upon the particular works your students study.

2 Lines

LINE EXERCISE 1: SURVEYS

Introduction

No survey is perfect. Polls include a margin of error for several reasons: the format of a question can bias the answer, samples of larger populations aren't always representative, and sometimes people just don't tell the truth. In the classroom, however, teachers always have to allow for a wider margin of error, in our students' work and our own. Error is sometimes the best way to learn.

The goal of the survey process presented here is not to gather error-free data but to spark discussion. The format of some statements may be a statistician's nightmare, but that's okay; as a teacher, I'm not trying to assess the overall opinion of a group but to present a challenge to the opinions of individuals: to engage rather than merely to gauge. It's in the discussion, not the compilation, that the response to such surveys becomes valuable to a teacher.

Take a look at the survey on the next page—you might even try taking it yourself. If you're like most students, you may want to talk about some of the statements before you even finish the survey. Resist the urge.

For each statement on the survey, circle the number (1–5) that best represents your point of view. Then add all of the circled numbers together at the bottom of the page. You should have a total as low as 10, as high as 50, or somewhere in between.

Sample Discussion Survey: Shakespeare's *Romeo and Juliet*

For each statement below, circle one number:

> *5—agree strongly*
>
> *4—agree*
>
> *3—undecided/equal balance*
>
> *2—disagree*
>
> *1—disagree strongly*

1. There is such a thing as love at first sight.   5 4 3 2 1

2. Love is ultimately a stronger emotion than hate.   5 4 3 2 1

3. Everyone in the world is destined to find one true love during his or her lifetime.   5 4 3 2 1

4. Love is uncontrollable; human beings are not able to choose the people with whom they fall in love.   5 4 3 2 1

5. Some illegal actions can be justified when they are committed in the name of love.   5 4 3 2 1

6. Love is worth dying for.   5 4 3 2 1

7. Ultimately, no marriage that is made for a reason other than love can be considered a true marriage.   5 4 3 2 1

8. It is better to give up being with one's family for love than to give up love in order to be with one's family.   5 4 3 2 1

9. Relationships built on true love are not weakened when the people in the relationship spend time in the company of others to whom they could be attracted.   5 4 3 2 1

10. One can feel true romantic love as a teenager.   5 4 3 2 1

Add your score   _____

Surveys: Guidelines for Use

- Have your class take the survey at the beginning of a class period. I find it works best to use the survey after the students have read part or all of the work we are studying. Ask students to complete the survey silently; discussion during completion may keep some students from processing the statements fully or may bias their answers.

- Once everyone has finished and has totaled their score (for my surveys, this is usually a number between 10 and 50), have the students form a large arc facing you. Point out that someone with a score of 25 should be in the middle of the room while a 10 or 50 should be to the far right or left side, respectively. If you need to move desks or tables to make room for the line, do so. If you need to shift the center of the Survey Line to make room for everyone, you can do that, too.

- After your students have lined up in order of their numbers, ask them what they think the two extremes represent. For instance, if you are using the *Romeo and Juliet* survey, you might classify a person scoring 10 as a realist and a person scoring 50 as an idealist (these terms themselves might serve to begin an interesting discussion).

- Ask your students to suggest specific items from the survey that they would like to discuss. As this discussion progresses, try to get students from different parts of the line to express their views. Balance the discussion by taking comments from students with low, medium, and high scores equitably.

- Point out some specific items from the survey and ask how they apply to the literary work in question. Encourage students to come up with specific textual examples.

- As you discuss scenes from the work, remind your students to consider their place on the Survey Line. Does this affect interpretation? Does it affect how much they like a character, scene, or the work as a whole?

- Question the statements on the survey. Are there certain words or phrases that change the meaning of the whole statement? How might responses to the survey statements change if it were given to a different group—a group of parents or teachers, for instance?

Notes About Creating Your Own Surveys

Surveys can be tough to make (though once you've made one, you've got a ready-made lesson plan for years to come). Because of this, I've included a few brief guidelines for making your own surveys.

- The trickiest part about making a survey is that the items on it—whether they're statements of theme, issues, quotations, or scene descriptions—must all *agree* with one another in some way. In other words, anyone who agrees with all of the statements is expressing a particular point of view, while anyone who disagrees with all of the statements is expressing the opposite point of view. It's not hard to make such statements work in a political arena, but it's tougher when dealing with literature or particularly complicated issues. Here's how I approach the task:
    * Think of an issue raised by the text with two opposing sides.
    * Think of ten aspects of examples or the issue that might be explored.
    * Construct a statement that expresses each of those aspects or examples in absolute terms.

- Two important hints:
    * Think about the overall issue both in general and specific terms. What might someone who agreed with all of your statements say, not just about specific instances but also about the nature of humanity or society?
    * I find it easiest to word all statements from a conservative point of view (that conservatism may be political or social). I find that such viewpoints tend to lend themselves more easily to absolutes.

- An alternative approach:
    * In some cases, the scale of answers might range not from "agree" to "disagree" but from one action to another. If you're having trouble coming up with statements that just require a degree of agreement, think about the issue differently: Is there an escalating range of options in terms of action? The survey dealing with foreign policy scenarios on page 109 works this way.

- A technical matter: Rather than "laying out" the survey yourself (that is, instead of trying to insert the numbers of the right side of the page in the middle of a statement), try dividing your document into columns. This makes later editing far easier.

Follow-up Ideas

As with most of the discussion methods in this book, the individual statements used in this exercise make good writing prompts or, with some modification, essay topics. It's never a bad idea to have students return to the text after a discussion, especially a heated or energetic discussion.

With a little preparation, you can usually guide a student's return to the text as a homework assignment or group activity to make it more profitable. A sample idea for following up the *Romeo and Juliet* survey with a short group project is included next.

Romeo and Juliet Group Activity: Views of Love and Marriage

Step One

Put your students into small groups. Assign each group of students a character who appears in act 1 of *Romeo and Juliet* (you can continue this exercise with the entire play, but the first act works particularly well):

Romeo	Paris	Capulet	Benvolio
Juliet	Mercutio	Lady Capulet	Nurse

Students should scour the text for any line in act 1 in which the character they have been assigned refers to love or marriage, directly or indirectly. Each group should then discuss the lines and come to a consensus about what the lines mean and how to characterize that individual's overall attitude toward relationships between men and women.

Step Two

Have each group share its findings with the class. I like to have groups write the name of their character, line numbers of relevant lines, and a brief summary of the character's attitude on a large sheet of paper that I can tape to the board. With younger students, I might allow time for an illustration on the poster, as well. When all groups have presented, you will have eight posters on your wall for students to compare.

Step Three

Through discussion or fast-writing, ask your students to consider the following questions.

- Where along the Survey Line might each of the above characters fall?
- Which characters above hold contrasting views of love and marriage? What complications in the plot might arise out of these contrasts?

- Do any of the characters hold views about love and marriage that surprise you? Which ones? In what way are their views surprising?

- With which character do you most agree about love and marriage? With which do you most disagree?

- Which of these characters change their points of view during the remainder of the play? How and why do they change?

As a final question, I often ask students to make a prediction about the rest of the work: What do they expect of these characters, of the plot, and of the work as a whole as they continue to read? Then, as we study the work, I refer back to the survey and the items on it. Sometimes, it turns out that a student has changed his or her mind about an item (or about several) as we read. What better way to illustrate the power literature has to affect the way we view the world?

Connecting to Current Events

Our tendency, I sometimes think, is to polarize the world in which we live: Ideas and issues are right or wrong, liberal or conservative, democratic or authoritarian. The real world is often more complicated, and a survey is a good way to allow students not just to find the gray area in a single issue but also to feel differently about different issues. Imagine, for instance, a survey on which a statement about making gun ownership illegal is followed by one about legalizing drugs—any given student might strongly oppose the first and support the second or vice versa.

In the last chapter of this book you'll find sample surveys that deal with current issues such as human rights, the role of government, and U.S. foreign policy. You might easily develop your own surveys for judging the political stances of your classes or their attitudes toward elections; you'll also find some additional guidelines in the last chapter for constructing your own surveys.

As you use such surveys, remember that any and all of these issues are relevant to literature; novels and plays often make good case studies for real-world issues and questions, and connecting literary themes to actual events makes literature relevant and exciting for students.

LINE EXERCISE 2: GET OFF THE FENCE

Introduction

The surveys described in the previous section are designed to help students recognize that not every issue is neatly divisible into pro and con sides. I'm very fond of Survey Lines that allow students to see degrees.

At the same time, some topics naturally lend themselves to polarization. Consider the following statement, which I once presented to a class of ninth graders who were studying *Lord of the Flies.*

> Human beings are born savage, evil, and monstrous; we must unlearn these traits as we grow in order to function in society.

A Survey Line may be an appropriate tool for the discussion of such a statement—it's easy to create a sort of minisurvey out of the issue by simply declaring that one side of the room is total agreement and the other is total disagreement and asking students to line up where they wish according to the degree of their belief in the statement.

But sometimes it's helpful to have a discussion tool that allows for an amount of division. A friend of mine dubbed this activity "Get Off the Fence" because of the twist that comes at the end (read the following guidelines to see how it works).

Sample Get Off the Fence Statements for Faulkner's *The Unvanquished*

- There are no moral absolutes; an action must be judged as right or wrong depending upon the situation in which that action occurs.

    Follow-up discussion: Throughout the novel, Granny wavers between moral absolutes and situational ethics. Discuss her reactions when Bayard and Ringo shoot the horse in "Ambuscade" and the horse and mule thefts throughout the novel. Ringo says of Granny in "Raid": "She cide what she want and then she kneel down about ten seconds and tell God what she aim to do and then she git up and do hit."

- When a large number of people are suffering, sometimes it is better not to help anyone than it is to help only one or two out of many.

    Follow-up discussion: In "Raid," Granny is faced with several situations in which she has to choose whether or not to help freed slaves. What are her responses to these situations?

- Revenge can never be justified; it simply perpetuates a cycle of violence that never ends.

    Follow-up discussion: At the end of the novel, Bayard refuses to seek revenge for his father's death, or at least achieves his revenge in an unusual manner. How do other characters respond to Bayard's actions? What message about revenge does Faulkner want us to take away?

- It is impossible for members of a social system that adheres to the institution of slavery to maintain a code of honor.

    Follow-up discussion: Many of the characters who own slaves in the novel—Granny, Sartoris, Drusilla, Bayard—adhere to some form of a code of honor. To what extent are these codes truly "honorable"?

- Any woman who acts in ways that are traditionally associated with males will be looked down upon by both men and women.

    Follow-up discussion: Drusilla rides with soldiers and refuses to wear a dress. How do other characters react to Drusilla? Ultimately, what message does Drusilla's situation send to the reader about life for women in this society?

- Because of the Civil War, no two people of different races in the South can truly be friends.

    Follow-up discussion: Are Bayard and Ringo friends at the end of the novel? Is it possible for them to remain friends in this situation?

Get Off the Fence: Guidelines for Use

- Offer your class a controversial statement about a work of literature by reading the statement aloud or writing it on the board.

- Ask those who agree with the statement to move to one side of the room and those who disagree to move to the opposite side of the room.

- Any student who is undecided may remain in the middle of the room, but those in the middle cannot speak. At any time a student may move from the middle to one side, from one side to the middle, or to the other side.

- Ask for comments from students about the statement, alternating from side to side.

- The unexpected ending: Ask the students in the middle of the room to "get off the fence" by choosing one side or the other, then explaining why they chose that side. No matter how reluctant or undecided a student may be, he or she must still choose a side (sometimes in life we have to choose sides).

- Repeat the process with another statement.

Notes About Creating Your Own Prompts

- Statements should be controversial enough that students will feel strongly about the answer. For this reason, I usually use general statements that sum up a major theme or an idea about a work, then follow up with a discussion of specific scenes relating to that idea (see the sample statements relating to *The Unvanquished*).

- I try to prepare several statements for one class period and switch statements as soon as I feel the discussion begin to stagnate.

- If you want to jump-start student ideas a little more, have the class fast-write in response to the statement before moving around the room. That way, everyone has a little ammunition for discussion.

- Don't try to come up with a definitive response to any one statement; there is not necessarily a right and wrong side.

Follow-up Ideas

So far, I've discussed two important ways to have students reflect on classroom discussions:

1. writing
2. returning to the text (finding lines or scenes that relate to a discussion topic)

Let me add a third possibility to the list.

3. discovering what others think about the issue

Try asking your students, for homework, to find out what those outside of the classroom have to say about the issue. The possibilities here are broad: you could allow them, for instance, simply to ask their parents or a teacher in another subject area for an opinion on the topic, or you could require students to find quotations from other authors or scholars (psychologists, scientists, literary critics, and so on.) that relate to the discussion. Have students share and discuss their findings with one another at the start of the next class.

Take, for instance, *The Unvanquished*. If you haven't taught this collection of seven consecutive and related stories, you might consider it; *The Unvanquished* is more accessible for high school students than many Faulkner novels and it contains a good deal of stylistic and thematic depth. The follow-up activity described above makes a nice assignment for this novel specifically: Students might research aspects of the Civil War, critical reactions to Faulkner's work, even Faulkner's own comments on his work (including his Nobel Prize acceptance speech). There are even other aspects of the novel to research: for instance, have students look up information about and make a family tree of the House of Atreus, the cursed house of Greek mythology. Then, in a class discussion, compare the characters of that house—Orestes and Electra in particular—to the characters in Faulkner's novel.

Connecting to Current Events

As well as having students find out what others think, you might use statements by others to spark discussion in the first place. Politicians and partisan commentators often make statements that beg discussion—how could one read conservative commentator Rush Limbaugh's "Thirty-Five Undeniable Truths" (easily found online) or excerpts from Al Franken's liberal *Rush Limbaugh Is a Big, Fat Idiot* without taking a side? In the last chapter of this book, you'll find a list of quotations from other political figures designed to provoke the kind of discussion described above.

An important note: I find it's best not to give students the sources of quotations until *after* the discussion. Many times, students will convince themselves that they agree with a statement just because of the speaker. If the speaker is unknown, they're more likely to think through their positions carefully, without particular bias. I *do* always give the source eventually, but sometimes only after several students have guessed about what the source might be based on the bias of the statements (a critical thinking exercise in and of itself).

LINE EXERCISE 3: THE GRID

Introduction

A few years ago a former student of mine asked if he could come and teach my class. Patrick had been to India and South Africa to study nonviolent protest movement, and I was eager for the students to hear about his experiences. But when he showed up before my class, moved all of the furniture to the sides of the room, and started putting down tape on the floor, I knew we were in for something different.

"It looks like we're about to play four-square," I said to him, thinking about the game from my childhood. Actually, I was pretty good at four-square, but I wasn't so sure how it would go over in my classroom, which is directly above the principal's office.

"Right," he answered. "This is similar, but there's no ball. And it's not a game. And it's not a competition."

"OK, so what's left?" I asked.

He smiled. "Fun."

Patrick divided the floor into four sections with two pieces of tape (he made a large grid like a plus sign on the floor). For his purposes, he labeled each quadrant with initials: VNG (for "violent" and "not good for society"), VG ("violent" and "good for society"), NVG ("nonviolent" and "good for society"), and NVNG ("nonviolent" and "not good"). When the students came in, Patrick posed a series of situations and asked us to stand in the quadrant that fit our attitude about the issue. I was fascinated and a little uncertain: Was a pillow fight violent? Were professional contact sports, like football, good or bad for society? How about shouting obscenities at another driver in a traffic jam?

I also immediately saw the value of the method, and I've been using it ever since for literature discussions. The quadrants change, but the idea is the same: to get students thinking not just along a line, but along two lines simultaneously, balancing judgments and considering value trade-offs in regards to literature.

The Grid: Sample Scenarios

Sample Work	Topic	Grid Quadrants
Hamlet	Characterization/ poetic justice	Good/Gets what he or she deserves
		Good/Doesn't get what he or she deserves
		Bad/Gets what he or she deserves
		Bad/Doesn't get what he or she deserves
	Students move and discuss after you read each character name: • Hamlet, Ophelia, Gertrude, Claudius, Polonius, Laertes, the Ghost.	
Lord of the Flies	Decision making/ sacrifice	Good for individual/Good for group
		Good for individual/Bad for group
		Bad for individual/Good for group
		Bad for individual/Bad for group

Sample Scenarios continued

	Students move and discuss after you identify each moment from the story: • Piggy suggests rules about talking and holding the conch shell. • Ralph builds shelters. • Jack has the boys hunt (instead of keeping the fire going). • The boys don't leave enough food at dinner for Piggy to eat. • Ralph tries to keep the fire going.	
Antigone	Just and unjust laws	Just law/Good for society Unjust law/Good for society Just law/Bad for society Unjust law/Bad for society
	Students move and discuss after you read each example: Start with general statements about contemporary laws, such as: • legal driving age of sixteen years old • legal voting age of eighteen • the death penalty for convicted murderers Move on to specific statements about the text: • Creon's decree against burying Antigone's brother Polynices • Creon's punishment of Antigone for defying the decree • the laws of succession that made Creon king in the first place • the laws of the gods requiring particular funeral rites	

The Grid: Guidelines for Use

• Before your class period begins, clear a space in the middle of the room and tape a grid (like a large plus sign) on the floor with masking tape. This part of the class alone is usually enough to generate energy—when students walk into the room, they're going to want to know what's going on.

- In each quadrant of the grid, tape down a sheet of paper on which you've written the appropriate two elements for that space—"Good/Gets what he deserves," and so on.

- As you read aloud each item or character from a prepared list, have the students move to the quadrant of the grid where they think that item belongs. Some students may want to stand on the line between sections—you can decide whether or not that's allowed.

- Take a comment from just one person in each quadrant. If no one is standing in a quadrant, ask the class whether anyone can come up with an argument that might fit that way of looking at the issue. After taking one comment from each quadrant, you might wish to open the discussion to other students as well. Encourage students to refer to specific scenes from the text as they make their points.

- Repeat the process with another statement.

Notes About Creating Your Own Grid Exercises

- With most other discussion models, the instructor needs to think only of an issue that elicits two opposing points of view. The toughest aspect of The Grid exercise is thinking of two issues, not one—and those issues need to coexist in situations from a novel. I find, therefore, that a grid is most suited to novels that intend to present a reflection of society and social issues, though purely literary issues such as poetic justice do work for this format.

- It helps to come up with statements that your class will actually discuss, so think through the prompts carefully: Have you come up with at least one that you could argue from the viewpoint of any quadrant? It's OK if there are a couple of statements that most people will agree on, but make sure a few are fairly divisive as well.

Follow-up Ideas

As you can see from the sample Grid activity involving *Antigone,* I often try to make classroom discussions relevant to today's society and the culture of the students. Grids offer excellent possibilities for such reflection and connection. Ask your students to think of other examples (news stories, people, school policies, and so on) that might fit into various quadrants on the grid.

Such reflection naturally lends itself to a homework assignment involving research and writing: Can your students find examples in the newspaper of people who made choices that were bad for themselves but good for society? Can they think of any unjust laws that are good for society (sometimes students in my classes like to argue that college admissions quotas fit this description)?

You might also use this activity as a springboard for connecting a work to other novels or plays you've studied. How does poetic justice play out in other works? How does the nature of the law in *Antigone* differ from the laws in *A Man for All Seasons, The Crucible,* or *Inherit the Wind*?

The connections, once you start looking, are often easy to find. The Grid exercise just helps spark the idea that these connections exist; make it a point to have your students follow those connections to other pieces of literature and the world in which they live.

Connecting to Current Events

The Grid exercise described above for use with *Antigone*—the one that combines a judgment about whether a law is just or unjust with a judgment about whether the law is ultimately good or bad for society—works well for a discussion of any number of contemporary issues. Here are a few examples of laws that could be considered just or unjust and also good or bad for society as a whole.

- affirmative action
- quotas or other weighted admissions systems for college acceptances
- random locker searches in public schools
- laws requiring drivers to wear seatbelts
- racial profiling at airport security
- rules allowing professional sports teams to recruit students out of high school
- Internet filters in public libraries
- corporal punishment administered by public schools
- capital punishment

The list could go on and on.

It's particularly important here, I think, to ask students to think about a possible argument for any section of the grid that might turn up empty in response to a given statement. There's almost always an argument to be made from every part of the grid, even if some groups find themselves more or less in agreement.

3 Circles

CIRCLE EXERCISE 1: THE FISHBOWL

Introduction

Over the years, I've come to believe that many teachers divide them-selves into "row" teachers or "circle" teachers. It's tempting to think, of course, that the teachers who arrange their desks or tables in circles are more creative and promote a sort of democracy in their classes, but I don't think that's necessarily true. Row teachers may be just as creative, give their students just as much choice, and make the classroom just as safe an environment as circle teachers—they may even do better in these areas.

Here's the challenge I offer to myself on a regular basis: Don't, I tell myself, be a row teacher *or* a circle teacher. Or, better: *Be* a row teacher *and* a circle teacher. It may mean lugging desks around the room be-tween classes, but it's worth it.

You may be surprised at how your students react to the change of scenery in your classroom. Sometimes they get irate. Sometimes they even try to move the desks back the way they were. And sometimes the change just doesn't work, and you wish you'd never changed a thing. It happens—the question is, Why?

Well, for one thing, it's not enough to stick kids in a circle and ex-pect them all to engage in brilliant and compelling discussions. They're often more likely to engage in pencil-tossing contests. If your classes are anything like mine, you probably still need some structure. I've heard teachers say that in a circle everyone is a teacher, but I've found the op-posite to be true: In a circle without structured rules, it may be that no one is the teacher, including me.

The Fishbowl is one of my students' favorite activities. They love it because it promotes equity, encourages participation, allows movement, and offers value to diverse points of view. They love it because it reduces me to just another participant in the discussion, one who can be shut up with the tap of a finger. And, I admit, they love it because sometimes I let them make fish noises to signify that they're finished speaking.

Fishbowls require controversial statements much like those I suggested for the Get Off the Fence activity in the previous chapter (examples for various works follow). A few weeks into the school year, I find I can often deal with anything contentious that arises, whether it concerns literature, school life, or life in general, by suggesting a Fishbowl. The students rearrange the desks and get to work with little prompting, and the result is almost always a more satisfying discussion—for them, at least—than they could possibly have if I simply stood in front of the class and posed questions, or worse, answers. It works because they feel ownership of the process, and of the discussion, because they buy into it, hook, line, and sinker.

The Fishbowl: Sample Discussion Prompts

General examples:

- Racial issues have been—and always will be—the most divisive issue in American society. *(To Kill a Mockingbird, The House on Mango Street, Invisible Man)*

- When a government controls what you hear, see, and read, it controls the way you think. *(1984, Brave New World, Animal Farm)*

- Left to our own devices, we all make decisions that are not in our own interests. *(Lord of the Flies)*

- Sometimes there is a difference between doing what is right and doing what is just. *(Of Mice and Men)*

- Change in society must start from the bottom up—with groups of the poor, the oppressed, the powerless, or the alienated—not from the top down. *(The Grapes of Wrath)*

- Everything is predestined; each person has a fate and no one can change his or her fate. *(Beowulf)*

Text-specific examples:

- *The Merchant of Venice* is not so much a comedy as a tragic exploration of the nature of prejudice.

- The lovers in *A Midsummer Night's Dream* are not truly in love at the end of the play, even though it seems as if the pairings have worked out neatly.

- Willy Loman from *Death of a Salesman* is not a tragic hero.

- Annie Proulx's choppy style of writing detracts from the overall quality of *The Shipping News* because it distracts the reader.
- The narrator of Tim O'Brien's *The Things They Carried* says he was more of a coward because he went to Vietnam than he would have been had he dodged the draft; he is right.
- Fitzgerald really did mean for readers to see the green light in *The Great Gatsby* as a symbol.

The Fishbowl: Guidelines for Use

- Put your students in a circle. Make a smaller circle of three to five desks within the large circle.
- Write a controversial/debatable statement on the board. Ask for volunteers to begin discussion of the statement; have these volunteers sit in the small inner circle.
- Allow the students to discuss the statement, following these rules:
  * Only the students in the inner circle may speak.
  * No student can be made to leave the inner circle until he or she has had the chance to speak at least once and to finish speaking.
  * After a student speaks at least once, anyone may tap him or her on the shoulder. A tapped student returns to the outer circle and the tapper takes his or her place.
  * A student may not reenter the inner circle until two minutes have passed.
  * These rules apply to the teacher, as well.
- When discussion begins to stall, change the statement or have students fast-write on the original statement.

Guidelines for Organizing Your Own Fishbowls

- Fishbowl prompts are very much like those used for the Get Off the Fence discussion presented in the previous chapter; you might refer to those exercises for some notes on constructing prompts.
- The Fishbowl method works very well when one or a few students (or the teacher) are dominating the conversation. Other students can actually force the talkative students to be quiet and listen for a few minutes. The teacher can always extend the time that must pass before a student reenters the circle.

- I'm not in favor, generally, of grading students for how they discuss, but it's fairly easy to give a participation grade based on whether or not each student enters the Fishbowl at least once. If the statement is a good one, however, this usually isn't necessary.

- Fishbowls often start off slowly; students are reluctant to be the first to tap someone out. Give them time to warm up.

- I tell students that if I get into the inner circle myself I usually just have a quick point to make and that I like to be tapped out quickly.

- I also encourage students to play devil's advocate—to get into the inner circle and argue points they don't necessarily believe or agree with. If I think students are doing this, I try to give them a chance to explain after the discussion is over.

Follow-up Ideas

In a good Fishbowl, a lot of ideas get presented quickly; these ideas are not always directly opposed to one another but may move off onto tangential arguments. Students find other ways of looking at an argument from those their peers have presented, and sometimes the conversation snakes its way backward, to points that have been made already.

I like to have students reflect on the exercise itself and the variety of ideas presented in it. I often ask them to write in response to the following two prompts.

1. How did the Fishbowl activity go today? How do you feel about the conversation as a whole?
2. Summarize the general viewpoints of the class. Which positions materialized most clearly?

Another way of approaching a debriefing of this activity is to provide one last statement for students to consider and about which to write. It helps if this statement offers an overarching idea, one that sums up many of the threads of the day's conversation. A quotation from a work or critic works well. I keep a stock of quotations that I can use for such occasions; I especially prefer those that ask students to reflect in a piece of writing on their own lives: "You must be the change you wish to see in the world" (Gandhi), for instance, of anthropologist Margaret Mead's assertion that we should "never doubt that a small group of committed citizens can change the world, indeed, it is the only thing that ever has." You can find more such quotations in an appendix at the end of this book.

Connecting to Current Events

Over the past several years, I've given presentations that are designed to promote understanding (and prevention) of the development of hate groups, the use of hate propaganda, and the steps to genocide. A Fishbowl discussion is almost always my preferred way of starting or ending such a presentation, for several reasons. First, such material is often disturbing, and discussion is a good way for students to process their thoughts and stay tuned in without getting overwhelmed. In addition, a Fishbowl can help students process information a step at a time—each statement can be designed to elicit thought about just one step in the series of steps that lead to such immense and almost incomprehensible tragedy. A Fishbowl also gets many students involved and comfortable, and students comfortable with each other and the class may find it easier to grapple with issues of hate and genocide. Here are a few of the statements I use to prompt discussion.

- There are some circumstances in which it is appropriate and acceptable to tell a racist or sexist joke.
- The most important step in combating racism is combating the use of racist language by any individual.
- It is natural and inevitable for humans to separate themselves into groups by race—and for those groups to conflict with one another.
- Feelings of hatred toward another group are always reversible.
- Genocide requires a belief that another group of humans is not, in fact, human.
- Genocide can happen in any society.

As always, these statements are designed to provoke response; more than ever in such a discussion, it's important for students to understand that purpose (and not for a minute to think you've used a statement because it's your own point of view).

The danger of a Fishbowl activity that is based on current events is that, because the teacher too is relegated to a smaller role, misinformation can be shared easily. You might set a rule that says that you'll interrupt if you need to correct an assumption or mistaken "fact." You might also provide some basic facts and figures for the students before starting, or have them look them up for themselves. Arguing from a position of total ignorance or misinformation often leads students to make easy assumptions but prevents them from thinking through issues completely.

CIRCLE EXERCISE 2: BRAINSTORMING GROUPS

Introduction

In most English classes, group work is a part of the daily routine. The problem with routines, though, is that sometimes they become, well, routine.

The strategy I present here is one I use when I feel that just putting students into groups is not enough. With tough classes, with bored classes, or with classes where group work seems to be getting monotonous for the students, I try Brainstorming. It's a simple activity, but with a little planning, the results can enliven an otherwise lackluster class.

A note: When I present this activity to groups of teachers, I always start by having them first list, in pairs or small groups, as many great couples (lovers) from literature as they can think of. What I like about this activity is not just the list we come up with, but how it energizes the room. Teachers like the exercise of drawing on a repository of stories that they love, and so do students. Every now and then, try using a little brainstorming as a jump-start for a completely different kind of lesson. Have your class, in pairs, come up with a list of movie titles that include an apostrophe before teaching a grammar lesson on possessives. Have them brainstorm a list of their favorite books from elementary school before teaching them a poem you loved in college. Brainstorming provides energy and connections at the same time.

Then, when you need students to make judgments about the items they list, try the specific approach to brainstorming described below.

Brainstorming Groups: Sample List Categories

General:

- topics for essay writing
- themes or symbols for a specific work
- quiz or test questions on a work of literature
- practice items for the PSAT/SAT
- adjectives that could be used to describe an author's tone
- rhetorical devices
- characters from all works your students have read that fit a single description (lovers, orphans, parents, confidants, outsiders, and so on)
- works students have read that discuss a specific theme, time period, and so on

- fishbowl, line, or survey statements
- opening sentences for essays on a given topic
- clichés to avoid
- possible college essay topics
- ideas to start a creative writing assignment (for example, a list of animals that symbolize something, a list of words to describe your hometown, a list of interesting colors, and so on)
- banned or censored books throughout history
- round or flat characters in a work

Using a specific text:

Pride and Prejudice

- key decisions made by a character
- scenes in which society treats a character unfairly
- moments when the narrator seems to judge a character or society
- examples of dramatic, situational, or verbal irony
- plot shifts in which the written word plays a role

The House on Mango Street

- Esperanza's similes
- characters Esperanza admires (and why)
- symbols
- moments in which Esperanza loses some degree of her innocence

Brainstorming Groups: Guidelines for Use

Note: These guidelines are designed to allow student discussion both in groups and as an entire class during a single period.

- Put your students in groups. You might try organizing these groups according to some related criteria (for instance, where students fell along a Survey Line). Groups should ideally be made up of odd numbers, preferably of around five students each.
- Discuss the Brainstorming activity with your students. Make it clear that brainstorming involves coming up with as many rea-

sonable ideas as possible—no judgments need to be made in the first listing of ideas. Unreasonable ideas are okay, too, although you don't want students to get too silly.

- Give the groups a subject for brainstorming and suggest a time limit (but don't stick to the time limit rigidly—play it by ear). Have each group choose a secretary to write down the list of ideas. Give the class a topic and let them start listing ideas.

- As the groups work, periodically ask how many ideas they have. Don't tell them they're competing—just hearing the numbers will make them work slightly harder.

- When the groups start to slow down, stop them. Ask them to count the number of items on their lists.

- If you're in a hurry, begin with the group with the most items. This will get things going, and I always find that the other groups still have items to add or ways to refine those already mentioned. If you're not in a hurry, you might start with the group with the fewest items on its list, then the group with the next fewest and so on. Have them read them out and write their list on the board as they read.

- Ask other groups to add only items that are not already on the board. When you finish, you should have a large list of ideas.

- At this point, there are a number of ways to approach using this list.
  - ∗ Discuss the list as a class.
  - ∗ If appropriate, ask each group to take one minute to decide on a single item they will veto (cross out from the list).
  - ∗ If appropriate, ask each group to take one minute to decide which item on the list they think is most important.
  - ∗ As a class or in groups, organize the list: What kind of sublists or categories might the ideas fall into?
  - ∗ Give the students another tangible goal—to write about certain items on the list, to create test questions based on the list, and so on.

A Word About Choice in the Classroom

One of my favorite aspects of the Brainstorming activity is the opportunity it offers for students to take control of the types of learning that go on in my classroom. Too often, I find myself dictating the structure of my courses, including everything from how we manage our time to essay topics, reading selections, and grading processes. Inevitably, when I step back and allow the students to make rubrics for their own assignments, set their own deadlines, choose the books they wish to read (within reason), select their own writing topics, and even schedule how we use our time together, I find that several benefits come about: The students become more invested in the course, their attitudes improve, their learning improves, and, more often than you'd think, they're harder on themselves than I am.

Brainstorming serves as a great step toward achieving a sort of quasi-democracy in the classroom. It begins when you let students brainstorm lists of topics for assignments, but the real benefits arise when you give students the opportunity to brainstorm in regards to the larger aspects of your curriculum. Before you begin studying a book, for instance, ask your classes to set the agenda by brainstorming, refining the list, vetoing certain items, and coming to consensus. What aspects of the book, you might ask them, are important to study? What does the class need or want to learn or discuss? How will assessment be accomplished? Set up some nonnegotiables before you begin to make your life easier—how much grading you, as teacher, can reasonably complete, some areas (like writing) that must be included, and so on. See if you can work together to complete a reasonable outline of the next unit.

The drawbacks? For one thing, it's a slower process. Brainstorming and consensus take time, but try to keep two things in mind. First, don't take shortcuts—don't put anything to a vote, or you'll lose some of your students and make the process a competition. Second, remind yourself that no matter how much time it takes, learning happens when students take charge of their own education, and sometimes it happens in wonderful and unexpected ways.

It's also possible that you won't get what you wanted out of the unit the first time you do this. You may really have wanted to work on rhyme and meter in poetry, even though your class chose to discuss metaphors and imagery. Talk about this with your class, but do it after the unit is over. Don't change the plans your students make unless they suggest the change (or at least buy into it). If you don't manage to cover all that you wanted to about a work or topic, use it as a learning tool, and see if things change the next time around.

Brainstorming and Student Choice—An Example

A few years ago, I tried a variation of the Brainstorming group activity described above. For this lesson, which took place in a class studying British literature, I wrote seven topics on the board, each of which indicated a body of literature I wanted to teach but might not be able to fit into our curriculum. The topics ranged from medieval ballads to twentieth-century poetry.

"This is the situation," I told the class. "Once we finish the literature we're already committed to read and study, we'll have one free week at the end of the grading period. We can study one of these seven areas of literature. I want you to choose which one we tackle."

I gave the class about half the period to do some quick research on-line about the various topics (as I recall, few students had even heard of "The Rape of the Lock," but several were eager to look it up. Sadly, after trying to access numerous sites that were, thank goodness, blocked by our school's Internet firewall—I should have known—one student looked up from the computer with a look of total disdain. "That's it?" he asked. "It's about cutting some girl's hair!"). Then, I designated seven places in the room for groups to meet.

"I don't care about even numbers," I said. "You just pick the group that represents the works you want to study." The students moved to various parts of the room—a couple in one corner, none in another, and a large group in the back of the room.

I instructed each group to brainstorm a list of reasons why the class should study that area of literature. Any reasons were acceptable—the material was fun, it was easier to read, it was shorter, it was more re-cent, it would be useful to them in college—whatever they thought. When each group had its list, I gave them two minutes per group to present their reasons to the class and convince the rest of us. After all of the presentations were finished, the class would vote—one student, one vote—and we'd be bound by the results. Because I was an interested party, I gave myself one vote, too.

The interesting thing about the assignment is that the group with the most students in it initially, the group arguing in favor of studying World War I poetry, didn't ultimately win the vote. The second largest group, the one supporting medieval ballads, won, because in addition to all of their other arguments they also got from me an agreement that I'd bring in my guitar and play some of the ballads for the class if we stud-ied them. I gave them my vote, too, even though I'd really rather have taught one of the other poetry units. They made a good case and de-served my support.

I'd like to say the unit was universally successful because the stu-dents chose the subject matter; in fact, it was fairly successful, though I distinctly recall that some students were more involved and more in-terested than others. Who's to say, though, what the response would have been had I decided the subject matter for the last week entirely on my own? For one day of class time, I purchased a sense of owner-ship and excitement from about half the class. Not a bad trade-off in my book.

Follow-up Ideas/Connecting to Current Events

One of my favorite topics for student brainstorming is democracy itself. In their groups, I have the students list the elements they think need to exist in a society or nation for a stable and legitimate democracy exist. Generally, after group listing and discussion, we come up with a list of between thirty and fifty "conditions for democracy."

That takes a full class period. The next day, there are all sorts of directions I might go. I might have students do online searches for lists of conditions compiled by "experts" (there are many of these available). I might engage students in a discussion about which conditions exist in our school and in my classroom, which conditions could and should exist, and what the obstacles might be to achieving democracy. In a literature class, I might have students write about the topic, or we might read an excerpt from Barbara Kingsolver's *The Poisonwood Bible* in which African characters react to Western-style democracy ("It seems odd that if one man gets fifty votes and the other gets forty-nine, the first wins altogether and the second one plumb loses"), or we might discuss the syntax of Kennedy's inaugural address or a similar speech from the canon of American literature.

What's most important is that I don't let the list go, that I capitalize on student ideas. With many discussion methods, the discussion can exist on its own, but with the Brainstorming activity, there's a tangible, student-created product that almost demands use. Save the lists your students create and try to bring them back later in the unit or even later in the year. The connections classes make to their own ideas can be the most valuable of all.

CIRCLE EXERCISE 3: IDEA PASS-AROUNDS

Introduction

Another form of brainstorming, the Idea Pass-Around, has one benefit that sometimes makes it irresistible to me: It's quiet. OK, so maybe that's not the primary criteria we should use to plan our lessons, and it's true that real learning is often noisy. But occasionally I want a lesson that offers the benefits of group work without the chaos. (For another great silent activity, see the Silent Discussion exercise in Chapter 4).

There are other benefits to this method, of course. It can be used, for instance, to ground students in the text on an individual basis while at the same time allowing them to bounce off ideas from others in the class. It assures a diversity of issues for later discussion. It can be used as an individual assessment tool.

And did I mention that it's quiet?

This is a particularly nice way to start a unit on a work or topic with which students are at least somewhat familiar. My most successful use of the Idea Pass-Around ever was on the day I started teaching *The Grapes of Wrath* with a group that read the book over the summer. I still pull out the nineteen pages of notes that class generated in one period and review them to make sure I haven't missed anything. In fact, I've included the main topics next—take a look.

The Idea Pass-Around: Sample Results

Because in an Idea Pass-Around everything—topics, examples, and all—is generated by students, there's no sample handout or list of topics to offer here. Instead, I've listed, just as the class wrote them down, the topics generated by students when we used this method to study *The Grapes of Wrath.* (This class, which was studying AP Language and Composition in conjunction with American Literature, was admittedly a good one.)

Below the list of topics, I've also included the actual responses of the class to just one topic—my personal favorite.

Student-generated discussion topics for Steinbeck's The Grapes of Wrath

- the character of Ma
- biblical allusions in the novel
- route 66 as a symbol
- the significance of grapes
- music
- narrative structure: Why the interchapters?
- scenes of violence
- male–female relationships
- communism and historical context
- Steinbeck's life and historical context
- homes, houses, and dwellings
- water imagery
- food and hunger
- roadkill—What's the deal with that?
- pacing and sentence structure
- Jim Casy as a character
- Tom Joad as a character
- dancing
- the "machine"—What's it a symbol of?

Here are the first few student responses taken directly from the sheet labeled "Roadkill—What's the deal with that?" (I told you it was my favorite—read on.) Keep in mind that the original paper was a mess of different handwriting styles, sizes, and colors and much more intriguing than a simple typed list. I've included asterisks between the comments from various individual students.

They're always trying to kill stuff with their cars—is that symbolic?

*   *   *

Yep. Symbolism = it's a tough life?

*   *   *

Chapter three—the whole thing is about that turtle. I think it's about perseverance . . . .

*   *   *

Compare that to page 252. Tom and Casy run over a rabbit and feel bad about it.

*   *   *

They don't feel too bad on page 252—they just keep talking about that car.

*   *   *

p 22—the rich woman tries not to hit that turtle but the truck sort of hits it without even meaning to—but aren't the rich supposed to be the callous ones?

*   *   *

It's like the machine—the truck just runs over things. The turtle is the Joad family trying to move on but can't because of the machine/big engine grinding them down without worrying about the individual.

Already, there are two scenes, some character development, and connections to other themes to discuss here, and though the topic is not the usual starting place, it will interest the students and provide a springboard to some important aspects of the novel, everything from pacing and syntax (in the third chapter, especially) to overall conceits and metaphors.

The Idea Pass-Around: Guidelines for Use

- Set up the desks or tables in your classroom so that everyone is sitting in one large circle. Make sure you have a spot in the circle, as well.

- Give everyone a single sheet of paper. If you're using this activity to study a text, it's nice for everyone to have the text handy.

- Give the students one minute to think of a single aspect of the work or topic that they think is important. After the minute is over, go around the room and have everyone say his or her idea out loud. If there's repetition, you can either ask a student to come up with another topic or leave the topic in the pool twice with the understanding that everyone will need to address that topic twice. Make sure that all of the topics are rich enough to support a number of points, opinions, or examples.

- When everyone has a topic, have each student write his or her own topic at the top of his or her sheet of paper. Then, ask everyone to find one specific example (I like to require a quoted line or page number in addition) that addresses that aspect of the work or topic. For instance, if a student's topic is the symbolism of water imagery in *The Grapes of Wrath*, she might find a scene describing the flood at the end of the novel, a rainstorm, or the river the family must cross to enter California. On the paper, she'd then very briefly identify the scene and quote a line or cite a page number.

- After most of the group has completed the above task, have everyone pass his or her paper to the right. Each person then adds an entry on the new paper, for that topic. Make sure you participate as well—add your own entries to each student's page.

- You can allow logjams or try to avoid them by setting a time limit, making a rule that any time a student has more than two papers waiting, that student can be skipped, or allowing students to help those sitting beside them. Try asking your students how they want to handle this before you begin.

- Emphasize the importance of adding a new idea or opinion to each page. Students can read each other's ideas—in fact, they *should*—and bounce off one another, but each entry should be new in some way.

- The exercise ends when everyone has his or her original page. You now have as many topics as you have students, with as many examples or subpoints for each as you have students.

- Collect all of the pages and photocopy them for every student, if that's reasonable, or type them and put them on a Web page, or copy them on overheads so that you can show them to the whole class.

A note: If your students have access to computers, the Idea Pass-Around can easily be conducted online through email, a forum page, or even by having each student start a topic on one computer and then physically move on to another machine—a nice way to integrate technology into your teaching.

Follow-up Ideas

Here are my favorite ways to use Idea Pass-Around notes.

1. Have each student review his or her own page and lead a five-minute discussion on it. What questions need to be asked? What aspects are troubling? How do the various examples combine to offer a big picture or overall meaning?

2. Use the topics as a starting place for essays. The evidence is already collected for the students, but they must formulate a thesis statement based on that evidence by themselves.

3. Lay the sheets of paper out on the floor or tape them to your board and have students group them in whatever way they wish. Then give each set of pages to a group of students and have them summarize that grouping and present their findings to the class. What overall ideas about the work or topic have they gained?

There are more possibilities—endless possibilities, in fact. The great benefit of this activity is that it produces so much information in so little time, and all from the students.

And, oh yes, it's quiet.

Connecting to Current Events

On September 11, 2001, I, along with the twenty-five students in my International Studies class, saw the World Trade Center being struck by planes and collapsing live on television. When the second tower fell, one student turned to me and asked a question that I'll never forget. She said, "That didn't really happen, did it?" It took me a moment to realize that the question was genuine—here was a student who genuinely did not believe that what she had just seen was real.

That one statement brought home to me the many difficulties that classes would face in the coming months and years. Amidst the many changes that followed the events of that day, my curriculum had to change, as well—not just in content, but in approach. It wasn't just that the students needed context to understand the situation, though my subsequent lessons did include a focus on contextual material such as geography, history, politics, and culture. In addition, students needed time for processing, for grappling with the tragedy of the event, the questions it raised, the doubts and insecurities, and the range of emotions that accompanied it.

On September 12, my class used an Idea Pass-Around to begin our approach. I chose the method for three reasons. First, it's a useful activity for organizing and approaching a complex subject, whether it's a novel or a war, into smaller and more manageable areas of study. Second, it allows students some voice in the direction of study; it allows them to choose the emphasis of the curriculum. Finally, it was a quiet, reflective way to begin to grapple with the questions that barraged them in the hours after the attack.

I began the Idea Pass-Around, in this case, with a question: "In order to understand these events, what do we need to know?" At the top of each sheet, a student wrote an area of study or discussion in answer. I still remember several of these. Some were informational topics, such as "What is the Taliban?" or "How did they get onto the planes?" and others required more psychological and sociological discussion. "What makes someone commit a terrorist act?" was one topic; another was "Why do people hate the United States?"

As we passed the papers around, I instructed students not to try to answer the questions or topics, but rather to add their own questions or ideas for how we might approach our study. Under the question "What makes someone commit a terrorist act?" other students wrote responses such as "People keep saying they were crazy, but are they really insane?" and "What role did religion play in convincing them to do this?" and "I think we should look at terrorists in this country, as well, and see if they're similar or different."

We left class that day with many more questions than answers (in fact, there are probably still more questions than answers about this topic), but I used those questions to organize our course of study over the next weeks. I chose the direction of study, but I did so through the students' questions and ideas, and every few days I'd write a new question, word for word, on the board, and teach starting with the ideas students had suggested themselves. The process allowed the class a sense of ownership and investment and made the unit more manageable—both mentally and emotionally—for all of us. This was a shared tragedy; it required a shared direction of learning.

Of course, the Idea Pass-Around works for topics other than an act of global significance, though it does work well for such large-scale topics. As an introduction to a unit, it might be used to decide how a class will approach the study of a country, a historical war or period, or an aspect of government such as, say, the legislature or the Constitution. Working through information students *want* to know more about rather than what a teacher thinks is important to students can be not just successful but a source of motivation, as well.

4 *Big Paper*

BIG PAPER EXERCISE 1: WALL POSTERS

Introduction

I always keep a supply of big paper in my classroom—poster-sized sheets—along with a large box of markers in assorted colors. It's true that any exercise in this chapter could be administered with regular sheets of notebook or blank paper, but I don't think the result would be the same. Something happens when groups of students huddle around big paper. They take the work more seriously; they can all see the paper and so participation increases; they just enjoy the activity more. And, too, the results of the work they do in groups is easier to display and share.

The trick with Big Paper exercises, I find, is to make sure that the poster, the paper itself, doesn't become the only goal in the minds of the students. It takes discussion to put the product together in groups, of course, but the main goal is to construct a basis for a broader conversation. Big paper allows for comparisons between the work groups do, for connections between the abstract and the concrete, for reflection on multiple aspects of the same issue. Though I try always to post the work students create on big paper in my classroom, I also try never to leave that work up for long. I don't want the class to get the idea that they have reached an end point in the thought process, but rather that new thoughts, new posters, are constantly emerging and taking their place in the spotlight for a short time.

The easiest way to use big paper is to make Wall Posters. On the next page, you'll find a specific activity I often use when I teach utopian and dystopian literature such as *1984, Brave New World, The Dispossessed, Herland,* or *Island.* You can adapt this assignment easily to create other imaginary locations that correspond with aspects of literature; rather than creating utopias, your students might create the ideal setting for a tragic play, a new world or society for a science fiction story, or the ideal set design for a production of a Shakespeare comedy. In the Guidelines for Use section for this exercise, you'll find more ideas of ways to use Wall Posters to teach literature and grammar.

A practical note: Big paper—the actual paper itself—can be expensive, especially the kind I favor, which has a sticky strip so that it can adhere to a wall without the need for masking tape. A cheaper alternative is to buy paper by the roll and cut it into pieces as needed. Either way, it's worth having some around, along with some markers and tape. Students like the variety. One student would joke each time he came into my room and saw the big paper materials ready: "If you can't broaden my thinking, at least you're going to broaden my handwriting."

Sample Wall Poster Activity: Create Your Own Utopia

It would be nice if utopias could exist without the practical limitations and problems of the real world. Most authors recognize that this isn't the case, and in novels that pose an attempt at creating some sort of utopia, the realities of human interaction and emotion generally lead from utopia to dystopia. This exercise is designed to allow students to grapple with this problem. Here are the steps I use:

1. Put students into groups and give each group two sheets of big paper and markers. Tell the groups that it is their job to create a utopian society, but that there are ground rules (these rules follow in the next steps).

2. Have each group draw a map of its utopia on one sheet of big paper, complete with any cities and areas of geographical importance such as mountains, rivers, jungles, deserts, or coastlines. The catch: The utopia must be located in the real world, and the group must be able to point out its location on a world map. Current political borders don't have to be recognized, but real geography does.

3. Have the group list the following information about its utopia on the other sheet.

   - the size of the population and some description of it (gender, ethnicity, and so on)
   - some overall descriptors of the society, including such aspects as religion, government structure, and policies about military strength and service, health care, social services, education, or the economy

- a "constitution" consisting of five laws fundamental to the society

4.   When the utopias are complete, ask each group to display its two posters and describe its utopia to the class.

5.   After all of the groups have shared, ask the class to discuss their thoughts about some of the following questions.

- What common elements do you see in the societies? Why do you think these appear?
- Which countries would function best in the real world and why? What problems would eventually arise in these "utopias"?
- In which would you most like to live and why?
- How did the groups work together? What problems arose and how did you overcome them? Is your method of working together reflected in the nature of your society?

6.   Return to your primary text. Discuss questions such as:

- What decisions did the author face in creating his or her utopia or dystopia? How did he or she overcome obstacles or problems?
- How does the society created by the author compare to those created by the class?
- Is a true utopia possible? Will all utopias eventually devolve into a dystopian state?

Utopian Literature: A Note

You might return to the Brainstorming exercises in the previous chapter as a way of starting a unit on utopian literature. See how many utopian and dystopian societies from literature your students can name. The results can be surprising and merit debate. Is *Paradise Lost* a utopian or dystopian work? What about *The Tempest*? Other works that students have mentioned in class: *We, The Beach, Sacred Hunger, The Giver,* and *Erehwon.* Even a simple search for information about the above works online will give students an idea of the breadth and variety of such literature, which in turn may enrich their understanding of a text they are actively reading.

Wall Posters: Guidelines for Use

There are any number of ways to use big paper for display in your classroom, and students almost always enjoy them more than group work without any definite, visible product. Here are several suggestions you might try:

Wall Posters

Before your students come to class, post several sheets of big paper in various spots around your classroom. At the top of each, write a general category—names of characters from a literary work, parts of speech, or themes, for instance. When your students arrive, have each one make an entry on each poster—a trait of the character, an example of the part of speech from last night's homework, or a scene exemplifying the theme. Use the posters as a basis for discussion either by discussing each with the whole class or by distributing one each to groups that can summarize and present for the entire class.

Alternatively, you might put students in groups and have each group create a poster for display, as in the Create Your Own Utopia exercise described above. Other worthwhile group Wall Poster activities I've tried: creating posters for the movie version of a work we're studying (this works nicely with Shakespeare plays, for instance); mapping the geography of a work of literature (try this with *Lord of the Flies, To Kill a Mockingbird,* or *The Grapes of Wrath);* illustrating individual stanzas/sections of a poem before we analyze it ("The Second Coming"); and writing individual quatrains and couplets that are then pieced together into a sonnet (the first and second quatrains must begin with "if," the third with "then," and the final couplet with "therefore"—try it).

Points of the Compass

Similar to The Grid activity presented in Chapter 2, this exercise divides a class into four groups: north, south, east, and west. Post a sheet of big paper on each wall of your classroom and label it with the corresponding point of the compass ("north" on the northern wall, and so on) as well as a category that fits the work you're studying. Probably the best example from my own teaching is a group of categories I used to discuss the style of early twentieth-century American writers, because the directions correspond to the writers themselves: under "west" I wrote Steinbeck, under "south" I wrote Faulkner, under "east," Fitzgerald, and under "north," Hemingway (by this time, the class had read works by all four of these authors). The associations were somewhat loose; in fact, I didn't actually suggest that students discuss *why* I'd identified the writers in this way. Instead, I asked students to choose a point and a writer on their own and, in the resulting groups, list any stylistic or content-related aspects of the writer's work that makes that work unique, interesting, or distinctive.

It's not really important for the points of the compass to have any re-lationship to the content of the posters, though. I've used the activity to have students discuss four aspects of a novel (characterization, theme, symbols, and style), to compare four characters, or to debate the main value literature offers to readers (entertainment, instruction, explanation of the unknown, exploration of the limits of the possible). I've even had students divide into groups to create sets of classroom rules based on what each student values most in a classroom setting (efficiency and pro-ductiveness, feelings and community harmony, structures and guidelines, or free-flowing and organic activities) or based on how students prefer to use classroom time (lecture, full-class discussion, group work, or silent in-dividual work).

In every case, the procedure I follow is the same: Students first choose a point of the compass and move to that spot. The resulting groups, no matter how large or small, work to create a list on the big paper—a set of characteristics, a list of ideas, or a set of ground rules, for instance. The groups then share with the class, and we discuss the merits and limitations of each point of view, possible compromises, and the reasons for the original choice each student made to move to a certain quadrant.

Unlike a Grid activity, however, the point of this exercise is not to provoke debate, but rather to allow students to work in areas in which they feel comfortable or in which they are particularly interested. It's worthwhile, sometimes, for a student to choose a character or an author he or she likes without competition—to know that it's OK for one per-son to like one character or author and twenty to like another.

The Jigsaw

Jigsawing activities offer an alternative to the standard group presenta-tion; here, students need not stand in front of the whole class and present formally. Rather, information is shared casually, in small groups. The concept is simple: Students work in groups with a sheet of big paper to create a list, an illustration, or some other product. Once all of the groups have completed their posters, one member of each group vol-unteers to take the poster to the next group, offer a brief explanation or description, and answer questions. This continues until all of the groups have discussed all of the posters. A full-class discussion might then prompt students to point out the merits of work completed by other groups in the class. Because presenters to other groups miss the material being presented to their home group, I sometimes build in time for each group to give the rotating presenters a brief summary of the material their group discussed, as well.

A second version of the Jigsaw activity involves a sort of specialization process. Students are assigned to groups, then number off within the group (this activity either requires having exactly the same number in each group or being creative with the assignment of student numbers). All of the 1s meet to discuss one topic, all of the 2s meet to discuss another topic, and so forth. Then, students return to their original groups, and the 1s "teach" the topic from their group to the others, followed by the 2s, the 3s, and so on. This works well with grammar topics (the 1s review comma rules, the 2s semicolon rules, and so on) or with short readings (the 1s summarize one sonnet, the 2s another, and so on). In this case, I sometimes give a sheet of big paper to every student and give them specific tasks. I might, for instance, instruct a group to list the rules for an area of grammar, three points that summarize a reading, or the form of a poem such as a villanelle on their big paper. The paper makes the process more fun and prompts better "teaching" by the students when they return to their original groups.

Advertisements

As I mentioned above, I've had groups create movie posters for works they've read. Advertising, with its unique reliance on both visual and verbal imagery, offers numerous possibilities for Wall Posters. Student groups might use big paper to write personal ads for characters in a work, to create book covers (don't forget to have them compose the blurbs for the back cover), to produce thirty-second television ads for a work of literature (acting is optional), to produce sample ads for products from a novel (*soma* for *Brave New World*'s audience or sources of poison for *Hamlet*'s), or to create gravestones for dead characters in one work or many. The resulting presentations are often as much fun as the group work itself (you might consider videotaping any that include acting).

Follow-up Ideas

Wall Posters can be saved fairly easily. Even better, students can type those that include only words into word-processing documents or PowerPoint slides that can be saved, emailed, projected, or printed at a later date. Saving student group work offers several benefits: comparison to later assignments, exam and test review, comparison to similar assignments completed by students in future classes, or just the chance to revisit ideas over the course of studying a work of literature.

Wall Posters that incorporate visual art, of course, should be displayed for a short time, at least (these continue to teach, as well). Classrooms in which student work is displayed—even upper-level literature courses—become spaces in which students feel some ownership and therefore more desire to participate. The artwork, by the way, doesn't have to be particularly *good* for this effect to take place. A few years ago, a group of students from a visiting school was engaged in an activity in my twelfth-grade classroom. Unaware that I taught in that classroom, one of those students looked around at the artwork on the walls and said, "I thought this was a *high* school." What struck me as interesting about that student's comment was what it betrayed about her expectations of high school. Isn't it possible for high school students to create, to have fun, and also to engage in a great deal of serious work, writing, and discussion? Do a few stick figures or drawings on the walls mean that less "real" learning is taking place in a classroom? I'd say no, as long as the visual imagery is the starting place for thought, discussion, research, and writing, and not the end product in and of itself.

The comment has become a running joke in classes I teach. Students enter, see the desks in groups or big paper on the walls, and say, grinning, "I thought this was a *high* school." The rejoinders are tempting ("You don't have to be high to be in school . . . ") but ultimately unnecessary; if the activity is a good one, students get the point that enjoyment and productivity are not mutually exclusive.

Connecting to Current Events

Create Your Own Utopia, the exercise offered earlier as a sample, works well when students are studying government, international relations, or laws and constitutions, as well as when studying literature. Other Wall Poster activities similarly lend themselves to a discussion of current events. Almost any topic can be used for Wall Posters or Jigsaw activities, Points of the Compass works especially well for the study of actual geography, and using big paper for the creation of advertisements is a ready-made lesson for teaching politics, propaganda, or economics and trade. Students might present a platform and candidate for a political party, for instance.

Adapting the utopia approach is easy, too. Students learn well when they must employ critical thinking skills themselves; that's exactly what happens when they must work together to come up with the ideal version of a supreme court (How should they be appointed? How long should they serve? How many members should there be?), a legislature, an electoral system, or a national budget. Similarly, you might have them design the ideal school or the ideal high school course—only by going through such a process will they really have to grapple with the value trade-offs and sacrifices such attempts involve.

BIG PAPER EXERCISE 2: COMBINING VOICES

Introduction

I'll never forget one day in my first month of teaching at my present school—the day I completely failed to make a lesson plan for one class. These days, armed with the activities I've learned and created and with a bit more self-confidence than I possessed early in my career, failing to make a lesson plan is not such a big deal; I usually have an idea of what I'll do in each class, but sometimes I still rely on trust—in students, in activities, in books, in myself—to make up the plan. Back in my first month, though, I still meticulously planned every class period.

The problem was this: My school had a rotating class schedule. There seemed to be no rhyme or reason to the rotation schedule, but no class ever met twice in a week at the same time. I now love this schedule, but at the time I was having enough trouble keeping up with which hallway my classroom was in, much less which class was coming next on Thursday afternoon. So it was inevitable, I suppose, that one day I would walk into a classroom just after the bell rang and realize that I was holding a stack of quizzes for another group of students entirely, and that I hadn't even *thought* about what my American Literature class was going to do that day. Twenty eager faces (well, if not eager, attentive, at least) watched me—I was the teacher, after all.

I took a long time to take roll that day, trying to come up with a plan, but my mind was a blank. We were between books, we'd just finished a creative writing assignment, there was no peer editing to be done. I had, I thought, *nothing* to do. (What I wouldn't give these days for a few more classes with *nothing* to do—we would do so much!).

I told everyone to get out a sheet of paper.

I told everyone to get out a pencil or pen.

I stood there and let them look at me for a moment.

"Okay," I said. "Draw poetry."

I let them look at me for another moment. One girl, Christina, finally raised her hand.

"Huh?" she said.

"Really," I said. "I mean it. Draw poetry."

"Like, draw a poem? One we've read?"

"No," I said. "I mean *poetry*. All of it—the whole kit and caboodle." And then, before they could get sidetracked on a discussion of just what a *caboodle* is, anyway, I added, "You can be as abstract or concrete as you want. You can be symbolic or literal. You can draw anything you want. But whatever you draw has to illustrate, visually, the concept—the entire idea—of poetry."

They looked at me like I was nuts. And then, miraculously, they started drawing.

The exercise was not really my own brainchild. I'd seen my friend Blanche Deaderick start a session in a similar way with one hundred students just that past summer; Blanche's exercise was better. She had students drawing the whole planet, with symbols and images of the current state of affairs in the world. It was a more concrete objective, and it produced, probably, better results. But I was desperate, this was a literature course, and poetry was all I could come up with.

Five minutes later, we had twenty individual pictures of *poetry*. I asked a couple of students to share theirs. One was a picture of stacks and stacks of books, another was a collage of images such as stars and musical notes and trees, yet another depicted a human brain divided into dozens of little sections labeled with words like *metaphors, diction,* and *rhyme*—a sort of poetic phrenology.

Enthused by their willingness, I took my next step from Blanche's session, as well: I formed groups. For the rest of the period, I followed the guidelines included below, resulting in seven posters hanging on the wall and a fantastic discussion about the nature of poetry. The next day, I brought in some poems about poetry—Archibald MacLeish's "Ars Poetica" and Nikki Giovanni's "kidnap poem" among them—and a week-long unit on poetry about poetry was born.

This wasn't great teaching, just quick thinking, luck, and a good class of students. But I've come back to this activity again and again, because it works. Combining Voices is an excellent exercise to use at the start of a course, as Blanche did, or with a group of students who are not acquainted. It demands a movement from individual thought to group consensus and requires the participation of each student in the group. The exercise also allows groups to draw upon individual strengths; there is a role for the artist, the presenter, the organizer, and the silent contributor.

There's another lesson embedded in that story, too. T. S. Eliot said that "immature poets imitate; mature poets steal." It's even more true of teachers—if only stealing activities from other teachers were the sole hallmark of one's maturity as an educator, I'd be pretty darn mature. I tell classes that all the time: "You're going to love this activity," I say. "I know, because I didn't have anything to do with making it up."

Combining Voices: Sample Activities

I admit it—"Draw poetry" is a bit vague as a class-starter. Here are some topical areas with specific examples on which you might base your own activities, along with sample related texts I've taught (many of these examples would work with numerous texts, however).

- *general concepts*
  - * the state of race relations in the United States *(Invisible Man, The Tortilla Curtain)*
  - * What it means to be a patriot *(The Crucible, A Man for All Seasons)*
  - * the role of religion in everyday life *(The Poisonwood Bible, Peace Like a River, The Grapes of Wrath)*
  - * what it means to be in love *(Romeo and Juliet, Ali and Nino, Pride and Prejudice)*
  - * the nature of war *(Catch-22, The Things They Carried, All Quiet on the Western Front)*
- *literary concepts*
  - * the nature of poetry, fiction, or drama *("Ars Poetica," MacLeish)*
  - * the role of the artist in society *(A Portrait of the Artist as a Young Man)*
  - * literary/historical periods, such as the middle ages or the 1960s *(The Canterbury Tales, One Flew over the Cuckoo's Nest)*
- *illustrations of aspects of a text*
  - * a character from the general prologue to *The Canterbury Tales*
  - * Esperanza's house from *The House on Mango Street*
  - * a possible set design for a production of *A Midsummer Night's Dream*
- *original text*
  - * lines of a poem or paragraph that can be pieced together into one group work

Combining Voices: Guidelines for Use

- Have each student draw a concept or illustrate a topic on an individual sheet of paper. You might try having students close their eyes and visualize the topic or concept first, then draw. Emphasize that artistic ability isn't really relevant—stick figures are fine. Encourage, too, total silence until everyone is finished drawing. There will be plenty of time to discuss the pictures.

- Once everyone is finished (this should only take a few minutes), ask two or three—but no more—students to share their drawings and explain them.

- Arrange the students in groups. Give each group a sheet of big paper and several markers.

- Have each group follow these steps:

  1. Every person in the group shares his or her drawing, with whatever explanation he or she wishes to offer.
  2. The group discusses how to compile all of the drawings into one larger group composition. Then, the group draws a new picture illustrating the topic or concept on the big paper. At least one element of *every* person's individual drawing must appear in the new illustration.
  3. When the poster is done, the group chooses one spokesperson to present the result to the rest of the class.

- When all groups are ready, call on them in random order to present their posters. Hang each poster on the wall as it is presented.

- Once all of the presentations are complete, discuss the overall impression the posters give. What similarities between drawings appear? What's most unusual? What truths, ambiguities, or questions about the original topic are raised by the posters? How might the pictures differ if they were drawn by a different group of students, a different age group, or in a different setting?

Follow-up Ideas

Combining Voices is largely an exercise in collaboration and compromise. Students shouldn't be trying in this activity to dissuade one another from a point of view or to debate issues; rather, they should be grappling with difficult concepts and ideas together, sharing inspiration, or just bouncing off one another's ideas. The activity is a good starter for a class for this very reason—the activity allows everyone a voice and a role without the stress of worrying that ideas will be shot down.

In that spirit, I often use this activity as a starter for a course, then try to build on the slight relationships built during the group work by pairing students, using the same groups for subsequent lessons, or just arranging seating in a classroom. It's also not a bad idea to follow up the activity with a fast-write in which students can discuss not only their ideas about the topic under discussion but also the nature of the group and the class, their expectations and hopes for future assignments, and any rules they'd like to see put in place for discussion (I keep such writing confidential, of course).

Used later in a course, this activity can be a nice breather from more "competitive" classes and can help generate discussion about a new and difficult or broad concept. I've used the activity, for instance, on the first day of a long unit on medieval literature by asking students to draw their visual images of the middle ages. The resulting posters made a nice starting place for a discussion about the difference between the romanticized castles and damsels in distress of fairy tales and the harsh reality of life, or about the vast changes that took place in the many centuries we label as "medieval." As always, having students write or research on their own at the end of a class period or as homework not only reinforces the ideas raised in the activity but offers students substance to contribute to future discussion, as well.

Connecting to Current Events

Some of the general examples in the sample activity above use the activity Combining Voices to explore current issues and events. At its best, the method offers a way for students to express both optimism and pessimism about society through visual means and small-group discussion, and then to discuss the delicate balance between hope and dismay, along with possible solutions to global problems, as a class. Race, religion, gender, politics—any or all of these groupings may be sources of conflict and of unity and celebration, and all may be tied to geography in a variety of ways. What, for instance, might the state of racial relations in your town or city look like to your students? What if you expanded the area to include the entire world?

An interesting twist on the assignment that works well with a study of current events and issues is to hand each group two sheets of big paper and instruct them to use one to draw a picture of how the issue currently appears and the other, a projection of how the issue will change over time. What will the racial state of the country look like in fifty or one hundred years? How will religion change the way we view the world during the next century? You can even ask some groups to illustrate the state of the topic in the past—to chart changes beginning one hundred years ago or more. The results may add to the general feeling of optimism or pessimism in the posters, and thus provide even more material for discussion.

BIG PAPER EXERCISE 3: SILENT DISCUSSION

Introduction

One of the greatest challenges for teachers of writing, I think, is communicating to students that writing itself is, in fact, an act of communication. In both casual and structured oral discussion, students are generally aware that an audience exists and that they are speaking to— or at least for the benefit of—that audience. Most English teachers try to impress upon students that an awareness of audience is just as important in written work, but it's a tough sell. Who is the audience for an essay, after all? The teacher? A couple of peer editors in class? Likewise, does the poem a student writes for homework ever make it beyond the in or out boxes of the teacher? It's all very well to talk about modes of discourse, but I sometimes catch myself asking students to write in different ways for different audiences when, in reality, I'm the only audience I provide for them (and, like it or not, they perceive me as a critical audience, because I sometimes must be).

Writing *is* a form of discussion, but the procedure is very different from an oral dialogue—not just in the process of forming syntax or revising, but in the very way we form and frame our thoughts. Writing slows us down, it highlights the grammatical inconsistencies we all use when we speak, it requires greater concentration and artistry, it offers enormous dynamic possibilities for expression. That's why English teachers love written assignments—and why students often hate them.

You could have students complete the exercise described below with a regular sheet of notebook paper (boring) or a computer screen (possibly better), but I've found that there's something about using big paper that changes how students respond. It's just not ordinary for high schools students to write on big paper with magic markers—it's colorful, it defies the rules, and it's fun. As simple as this activity is (and it's probably the simplest one in this book) students enjoy it, I enjoy it, and it has visible results.

Starter Phrases: Silent Discussion

Students work in pairs for this activity. I like to use starter phrases—the first partner actually writes the phrase down, word for word, and then completes the thought to kick off the Silent Discussion. If the discussion is literature-based, I sometimes encourage, or even require, partners to include specific examples from the work (this often means that the student who is not actively writing spends the waiting period looking up quotations or scenes). Here are some simple starter phrases that work with almost any age group:

- My favorite character in this book is _____ because . . .
- Here's what I learned from this book:
- I would have enjoyed this book more if the author had . . .
- If I could say anything to the author of this work it would be . . .
- Another work this book most reminds me of is _____ because . . .

The list is endless. Likewise, getting students started on a possible creative assignment (related to literature or not) is easy using a starter phrase. I generally try to ground students in their own pasts and to encourage them to write about what they know (even if they've forgotten what they know).

- I remember the first time I . . .
- I got into really big trouble with my parents the time I . . .
- The worst pain I ever felt was from . . .
- My most prized possession is . . .
- The person in my family with the most interesting hands is . . .

Combining the above types of phrases works, as well. Have students write about their own houses ("My favorite thing about my house is . . . ") before reading *The House on Mango Street* or *Howard's End*, or about jealousy ("The most jealous I ever felt was . . . ") before studying *Othello*.

Silent Discussion: Guidelines for Use

- Put your students into pairs. Give each pair one sheet of big paper and two differently colored magic markers.
- Write a topic or starter phrase on the board.
- Instruct the students to choose one partner to begin writing. This student can write anywhere on the paper, at any angle or in any direction. Normally, I don't need to set a time limit (minimum or maximum), but with a reluctant or overly eager class that might be a good idea.
- When the first partner is finished with his or her thought, the second partner should begin writing—an answer, a question, a new idea on the same topic—whatever. Make sure the second partner writes in a new color.
- Emphasize that at all times both partners, the writer and the one waiting to write, must remain absolutely silent. No one in the room is allowed to speak.
- Have the partners trade until they fill up the paper or time for the activity elapses. With a good prompt, most students will keep writing for as long as you wish them to.
- If you wish, allow time at the end of the activity for sharing. I like to share the discussions silently, as well, by laying them on desks or taping them to the wall and have students move silently around the room, reading the conversations others have had (if you wish to preserve anonymity, tell students not to write their

names on the paper and mix them up before posting them for the whole class).

Notes About Organizing Your Own Silent Discussions

- If you've ever watched a class of students writing, you know that it takes longer than you'd think to write a sentence by hand. Students themselves don't always realize this, at least until they're sitting quietly waiting for someone else to finish his or her thought. There are a couple of benefits to this. One is the possibility of discussing patience as a part of writing, the merits and drawbacks of handwriting as opposed to typing, or the physical act of writing itself—an aspect of writing we often neglect after elementary school. An even greater benefit, though, is the fact that the waiting partner, the one who isn't actively writing, generally starts to reflect on the topic while waiting. When the activity is over, many students will realize that the waiting period is not, in fact, a period of inactivity, but a period of mental activity that makes one ready—if not downright impatient—to start writing again.

- You might not wish to make a point of it, but grammar and spelling aren't necessarily the object of this lesson. If you feel the need, have students correct grammar or spelling errors *after* the conversation is finished.

- As with any conversation, there's often a certain length of time that it takes to cover a topic adequately. The trick for the teacher is judging this length of time and stopping before conversations peter out or become redundant. Stopping the conversation in a timely manner will also keep students from getting bored.

- You can enlarge groups by using multiple topics—two topics on two sheets of big paper shared among three students, for instance.

Follow-up Ideas

The Silent Discussion is essentially a fast-writing exercise—a chance for students to get ideas down fairly quickly with some freedom from the constraints of prepared writing that will be graded eventually, although there is some time for reflection built into the activity. As with all fast-writing, however, the first product is likely to be general, to range over a variety of possible topics, and to offer hints of ideas and stories that are not fully explored.

One of my goals as a teacher of writing is always to encourage students to be detailed and to explore the minute and concrete in their writing—as one writing teacher of mine put it, not to leave out the "furniture" of a poem, story, or essay. In creative writing, this furniture is often the specific objects, textures, and sensory features of a scene or story; in essays, it's the analysis of individual lines or words.

One follow-up technique that helps students get at these details is a kind of layered writing (you can use this technique for revision of individual first drafts or fast-writes, as well). After the first conversation is complete, instruct students to read through the discussion again and circle any five words or phrases that suggest a further story, idea, or topic. In a Silent Discussion activity, partners might circle only words written down by the other partner in order to help that student filter the material.

Next, have each student choose just one of his or her circled words or phrases and complete a second fast-write just on that object, story, or topic. You can repeat this process an infinite number of times, in theory, but generally once or twice is enough to start getting a more detailed level of thought, analysis, and description. At the same time, the act of rewriting may help tighten the overall style of the student's work.

Ultimately, the writing should move toward a finished product—a poem, a story, an essay, an informal discussion of an aspect of a work of literature. The lessons for the student, of course, are that the best writing, fiction or nonfiction, rarely occurs in the first draft and that detail almost always strengthens written work. The above process may take one class period or several. Sometimes letting the ideas and written words percolate for a day or so helps a student approach a next draft.

Connecting to Current Events

In an earlier chapter of this book, I described where I was when the World Trade Center was attacked in 2001. For some time, students will remember this event, as well—they'll also remember other major world and national events. Silent Discussion offers a way for students to share reactions and thoughts about such events and to personalize them; you might start a session with the prompt, "When I first heard about the terrorist attacks of 9/11, I felt . . ."

You can also use the activity to start a discussion about almost any current policy or issue. Offer the first student to write the permission to take either side on an issue by beginning either with the phrase "I support _____ because . . . " or with "I oppose _____ because . . ."

Such discussions, of course, emphasize emotional response over factual understanding, and should be used accordingly. Silent Discussion is a particularly useful activity for starting a unit of study and for encouraging personal connections to academic information.

5 Technology

TECHNOLOGY EXERCISE 1: THE ELECTRONIC CONVERSATION

Introduction

Beginning a year or so ago, my school began a laptop program: now, every student owns and brings a laptop computer to class, where each also has access to wireless internet, email, and a printer. It's a privilege most schools and students don't dream of, and for several years before the program started I'd been absolutely dreading it.

I'm not a Luddite, but I have certainly been a skeptic. I tried using PowerPoint to teach and for student reports, and I disliked it—too many bells and whistles, not enough substance (nothing is quite so boring as listening to a student read words you can already see on a screen). I've seen the grammar exercises and quiz programs that are available to teachers, and they often seem little better than electronic versions of the worksheets from books I stopped using long ago. Online resources will be helpful to students, but nothing—and I mean *nothing*—can replace a paperback copy of a novel in the hands of my kids for sparking a discussion.

But I'm coming around.

To begin with, my own experience suggests that students who type their written work tend to write more and to compose more complex sentences than those who only write by hand. Electronic composition may increase the time students spend on written assignments, their attention to detail in writing, and the sense of accomplishment they feel with the completion of an assignment. What's more, having students type their work helps me grade faster and more easily, and anything that helps me reduce the piles on my desk is a good idea in my book.

So sure, except for the timed essays AP students write or practice essays for the SAT, it makes sense to have students type their essays and creative pieces. But computers in the classroom? I've never quite been able to picture it. The logistics aside, how do I know two kids aren't playing games or instant messaging one another in the back of the room? How do I control the use of spell check or combat plagiarism from the Internet?

Coming to Terms with Technology

Some of these issues are still hotly debated in our school. But in my own quest to integrate technology into my English classes, I've had to do a lot of thinking about how computers can—and can't—benefit students. There are, of course, numerous ways in which computers can augment those things I already do; I already add images in PowerPoint presentations to my lectures (and I've come up with some better rules for PowerPoint as a tool in student presentations, such as limiting the number of words they may use on a slide and having them time slide shows). I also have students complete research on the Internet and I use a website to post my homework assignments each week. I'm more concerned, however, with the role technology will play in the basic elements of my curriculum—reading, writing, analysis, and discussion. I don't want PowerPoint or websites to replace the formal essay or word processing to replace oral dialogue, though I recognize that these tools may augment those activities.

I've tried, therefore, to consolidate my thoughts about the benefits of teaching with computers into a few points. I believe that these are relevant whether I am teaching in a room full of computers or in a room with one.

- The goal of the teacher should be to use technology mainly in ways that enhance the curriculum by offering activities that cannot be completed *without* technology. Although there are some useful programs that can simply replace similar tasks that I've traditionally done on paper, that's not the best use of computers in my classroom (though it's not an unacceptable use, either).

- It's better to embrace the way students write online than to combat it. Online discourse is closer, in many ways, to oral conversation than it is to handwritten work. The vocabulary and syntax of online discourse need not replace the formal writing I expect of the students; to the contrary, they need to understand that modes of writing appropriately alter according to purpose and audience.

- Typing can improve student writing and facilitate student thinking. Students with strong keyboarding skills will often find that typing is a happy medium; they must take the time to formulate thoughts carefully, but are not hampered by the tedium of handwriting.

- Students are more likely to revise when working on computers.

- Technology offers students opportunities to organize material in a linear, logical fashion and also to make creative leaps and horizontal links from idea to idea and from one written work to another. Both of these abilities are important for a sophisticated writer and reader.

- Technology offers students an interactive forum in which the written word can coincide with discussion.

Putting these beliefs into action in a lesson plan isn't easy, but before the students ever got laptops I tried assignments on classes that involved technology as a tool to improve—not replace or simplify—student writing. The following is an example of a lesson that can be used with any class that has access to computers at home, in a lab, or in the classroom.

The Electronic Conversation: Sample Activity

Last year I taught *A Tale of Two Cities* for the first time. As I read the book again, I was struck by the number of recurring images and symbols that Dickens includes. Normally, I might have devoted a day or two of class time to student group work. Probably, I'd have asked the students to discuss an image or symbol thread in groups, have one person write down notes, and present their findings to the class. This approach works well enough but is never quite satisfying to me, because the presentations are usually dry and the notes scanty. Last year, I tried something different—the Electronic Conversation. I put students into groups of three or four and had each group follow the guidelines for use that you'll find at the end of this activity. Following are some specific examples from this particular assignment.

The Early Process: Choosing Topics

Groups were instructed to choose a recurring image or symbol from *A Tale of Two Cities*. A few of the topics last year's groups chose: blood and wine, resurrection (literal and figurative), footsteps and imagery of feet, water imagery, animal imagery, balances, and pairs. Each of these topics easily yielded ten or more passages from throughout the novel.

The Electronic Conversation: An Excerpt

The results of the Electronic Conversations were surprising. I'd made the assignment partly as a way of saving class time (it did), but what I didn't expect was that the conversations would turn out to be interesting, productive, and enjoyable to the students. Moreover, most of the groups, after using some form of instant messaging or chat rooms for a conversation, turned in around eight to ten pages of text—far more than they were required to produce. Here's an uncorrected sample from one group's transcript, beginning with a quotation from the text:

SARAH: but, the time was not come yet; and every time that wind blew over france shook the rags of the scarecrows in vein, for the birds fine of song and feather, took no worning. book 1, ch 5

MARK: ok . . . what does that mean?

TAYLOR: the scarecrows are the aristocracy

CLAIRE: once again the birds are dirty

TAYLOR: i think

MARK: wait a seec

Claire: no,no,the wind is the scary mean people and the scarccrow are the porr people fighting the revolution

SARAH: yeah Claire that's what I was sayin

CLAIRE: and rthe poor are scarred away until the revolution comes

MARK: I think that there were so many times the thwe revolution could have occurred that (wind in vien) that when it actually cam the rich had no idea it was coming

When I discussed the assignment with my classes, they agreed that this conversation was different from any they had previously had about a book. The messaging format, they told me, forced them to react to one another as they would in a conversation, and at the same time to slow down enough to think through the way they would phrase a point or complete a sentence. They also enjoyed the discussions. Several of the groups meandered a bit, got off topic altogether, or wrote notes to me intentionally, but that didn't detract from the overall quality of the conversations.

Conversation Summaries: Sample Passage

Here is a passage from the summary of the group whose conversation I included above.

Although the barbaric human is often mentioned, we feel that the most important thematic issue within animal imagery is how the poor people are referred to as dogs and pigs. But social class differences are also illustrated symbolically by other images, such as the description of the ragged scarecrows (symbolizing the poor), while birds symbolize the upper class.

Clearly, the discourse had changed. The group was aware that this product required a different tone, level of grammatical correctness, and organization than the online chat.

The Final Product: Formal Essays

The essays the students wrote were good. Were they better than usual? Perhaps slightly. But what I liked about this assignment was that the students were eager to write the essays, were able to write them more quickly than usual, included a great deal of textual evidence (after all, they had compiled most of it already), and made interesting connections between scenes that sprung from paying close attention to the discussion results of the other groups. Moreover, I liked the fact that the students had to move between modes of discourse, to revise informal text into formal text. Here is a paragraph in which the ideas generated by the above assignments appear in one student's formal essay.

> In addition to the obvious use of imagery as a way of categorizing social groups, Dickens uses such symbolic language to foreshadow the coming revolution. In portraying the broken wine cask early in the book, he offers a general statement of "warning" for the reader that is wholly missed by the aristocracy, who, like "birds fine of song and feather," go about their usual business heedless of the coming turmoil.

The above assignment proved to me that students can work in multiple modes of discourse within a single assignment. Moreover, it showed me that the discourse of one familiar medium can actually augment my students' expository writing. Best of all, this use of technology scored highly on the best gauge I own as a teacher, however unempirical it may be; when we finished the last revisions, one student asked, "Can we write essays this way again next time?"

The Electronic Conversation: Guidelines for Use

- Put your students into small groups of three or four people each.
- Have each group choose an image or symbol that recurs throughout the book you are studying. (You can modify this assignment so that each group chooses a theme, character, stylistic device, or setting.)

- Instruct each group to compile a list of scenes (with page numbers and brief descriptions or explanations) in which its topic is evident. The lists should include around ten scenes. Note that the group needn't discuss the scenes at this point; they only need to identify them. This step can be completed in or out of class. Students can split up the job or work on it together.

- Give the class these instructions:

  Sometime during the next week, you must conduct a written Electronic Conversation on the topic. In this conversation, your group should discuss the thematic connections and the function of your topic. In other words, you should use this forum to brainstorm ideas about how and why Dickens used a certain thread of imagery or symbolism as if you were preparing to write an essay about your topic. There are several ways you might accomplish this.

  * Exchange emails between members of the group.

  * Arrange for an online conference using a chat room.

  * Use one of the computer lab computers and type responses to one another over time in the same Word file.

  Your conversation must include at least five substantial contributions from each member of the group (you may include many more short contributions instead). The total conversation should be at least three to four typed pages in length. Turn in a typed transcript of your conversation one week from today.

- Respond to the student conversations. Instead of writing comments on the hard copies of the conversations, I like to continue the electronic thread of the assignment by emailing students my own responses to their conversations, a technique on which I've since grown dependent, as I can include many more comments more quickly when I type.

- Have each group, as a group, write a summary of half a page or so in which they explore the overall thematic issues of the conversation. Summaries may refer to specific scenes, but should focus on the big picture—how the various threads of theme, imagery, and symbolism tie together and what overall message or meaning the author wishes to convey. What complexities or subtleties about the connections between these scenes are important to understand? Have the groups hand in (or, better, email) the summaries to you.

- Make *all* of the summaries available to students. You could choose to photocopy the summaries and hand them out. I post them on my homework website along with the guidelines for the assignment and the original lists of scenes from each group. The students have several days to look through them.

- Have each student, individually, turn in a typed, formal essay. The prompt I'd suggest would ask students to tie together the aspect of the book they've discussed (a symbol or image thread, for instance) with a major theme or the overall meaning of the work. Students may write about their own group topic or one of the topics from another group, using ample evidence from the text.

Follow-up Ideas

The process of using technology to help student writing doesn't end when a student turns in an essay. My classes revise every essay they write (see the section in this chapter titled Tracking Changes for some ideas about using technology as an ongoing part of the revision process). Once students get used to the idea of online discussion and using technology to develop and revise writing, the possibilities for further discussion increase greatly—group work can continue beyond the classroom. A group might simply hold a chat online as homework, partners might email one another to share brainstorming ideas for future assignments, or students might even form chat groups between classes to share and compare information. There are numerous assignments through which you can formalize and embrace the methods of communication and discourse students already use.

Students in my classes will not stop handwriting certain assignments. I won't forego printed books for e-texts or class discussion for hours spent alone with computers in class. I believe, however, that it's my responsibility to explore the ways in which technology can enhance and augment my curriculum, to continue to seek ways in which the computer can improve the basic skills I've taught in more traditional ways in the past.

Connecting to Current Events

An Electronic Conversation, of course, can focus on any topic—literary, political, or social. It's easy to use the same discussion format to have students discuss and write about contemporary issues. In addition, such a discussion can easily be enhanced by using technology as a resource in another way—for research. Although it's wise for students to be wary about the amount of misinformation available on the Internet, the existence of the Web makes it possible to study current events through a wide variety of viewpoints and sources, many of which provide information in an immediate fashion.

Substituting global issues for a literary text, for instance, is fairly easy. Instead of finding ten scenes in a novel, students might start by gathering ten websites that explore human rights abuses in China, the spread of AIDS in Africa, or homelessness in the United States. After gathering multiple websites, students can use an Electronic Conversation to filter through conflicting information, make judgments as a group about the legitimacy of the sources, and try to reach conclusions about the issue as a whole. The rest of the activity can proceed according to the instructions above; written work and group presentations are natural products of such a method.

TECHNOLOGY EXERCISE 2: IN THE FORUM

Introduction

An online forum differs from a chat room in the same way a suggestion box differs from a live person behind the desk of a complaints department—the dialogue is less immediate, but the opportunities for considered reflection and response are greater. For teachers, there are numerous additional reasons to use a forum on which each student can post a response at his or her convenience: schedules don't need to be aligned, no one can be interrupted while trying to make a point, multiple topics can be organized neatly and easily, the quantity of written response is easy to assess, and there are no concerns about technology being compatible, as long as each student can access the Internet. The drawback, of course, is that interaction between students is stiffer and a bit less natural; the forum is not a replacement for a group discussion but an alternative to it.

Another major benefit is that there are numerous sites that offer free use of an online forum, and they are often extremely easy to set up and access. The sample forum discussion featured on the next page is a generic example very similar to any number of sites you might find through a quick search online.

A forum is a fine avenue through which to extend group work beyond the limits of classroom space and time, but a forum is particularly useful in the same way wall posters are useful—both can lead students to juggle multiple topics at once. The exercise presented in the guidelines for use is of this sort, and the follow-up idea at the end of this section suggests a use for the assignment that can broaden your classroom significantly by including multiple classes or even multiple schools in the conversation.

In the Forum: Sample Discussion Page

Below are samples of a recent forum exercise from my own classes. I've simplified the format slightly, but these examples include the essential information and layout of the original site. Students in this class chose to read one of four works independently (each work is related to other material in my curriculum in some way). Then, each student logged on to a forum I'd prepared in advance. The first page of the forum contained a section that looked like this:

Forum	Topics	Posts	Last Post
God of Small Things	5	87	Guest, April 7, 2005
Grendel	5	69	Guest, April 8, 2005
The Piano Tuner	5	81	Guest, April 7, 2005
R&G Are Dead	5	74	Guest, April 7, 2005

Imagine you're a student in my class and that you chose to read Arundhati Roy's *The God of Small Things*. After logging in and reaching this screen, you simply click on the title of the novel above (also the title of that forum). The next screen you see offers a list of topics, each of which designates an AP-style essay prompt I've already posted, like this:

	Replies	Author	Last Post
Travel	16	Gilmore	Guest, April 7, 2005
Water Imagery	8	Gilmore	Guest, April 7, 2005
Parents and Siblings	4	Gilmore	Guest, April 7, 2005
Politics	21	Gilmore	Guest, April 7, 2005
Language and Style	17	Gilmore	Guest, April 7, 2005
Humor	19	Gilmore	Guest, April 7, 2005
The Symbolism of Names	26	Gilmore	Guest, April 7, 2005
Alienated Characters	23	Gilmore	Guest, April 7, 2005
Belief Systems	9	Gilmore	Guest, April 7, 2005

Your assignment is to respond, with specific references to the text, to any of the above prompts. You must submit at least six posted responses in all. Because the first prompt looks as promising as any, you click on "Travel," and you see the prompt plus some replies from your classmates (who have identified themselves by initials only):

	Post Reply
Author	**Message**
Gilmore (admin) Posted 4/1/05	Authors have often found that physical travel between locations in a work can serve to enhance that work's themes and the development of characters. Choose a work of literary merit (in this case, use *The God of Small Things*) in which a journey or journeys is crucial to the reader's understanding of the overall meaning and, in a well-organized essay, discuss how the journey helps to create that meaning. Avoid plot summary.
	Post Reply
Author	**Message**
c.a. Posted 4/5/05	I would talk about Estha's journey away from the family and then coming back, and how he doesnt talk throughout his journey. Also Sophia Mol's journey to visit, and then she ends up drowning.
m.l. Posted 4/5/05	The family's journey to see The Sound of Music provides a lot of insight to the overall meaning of the story. They see many characters along the way from their past. Also, many of the events that happen on the journey and once they have reached their journey affect the lives of all of the characters.
r.b. Posted 4/5/05	I hadn't thought about the movie trip—I was thinking of big international trips like Rahel going to America. You're right, tough—the orangelemondrink man is the most important point in the novel, so that trip is the one to discuss. Thanks!

| | Post Reply |
Author	Message
j.b. Posted 4/6/05	How about Sophie Mol's journey . . . eh? her journey into death? think about it
f.h. Posted 4/6/05	Um . . . maybe. Too abstract for the question, maybe. I have to say that Rahel going back home is like her returning to her past, her brother, and her family . . . India represents Rahel's true identity. She leaves her American identity behind when she comes back home.
g.g. Posted 4/7/05	there are a few posts about this. A significant journey in this story is that of Rahel. She goes through a physical journey when she leaves her home in India and travels to America. Also, she goes through a journey of separation from Estha and then being reunited with him in the end.
r.b. Posted 4/7/05	Back to the Sound of Music trip—because I agree with you guys about Amercia, but I still think that's richer material. It's not just Estha who changes but also Rahel—her mother loves her a little less, etc.—that's the way to go, I think.

To complete the assignment, you click on "Post Reply," add your two cents, and move on to another prompt. See the guidelines for use in this section for more specific information about this process and the follow-up to it.

In the Forum: Guidelines for Use

- One of the most important aspects of the online forum is the ability you and your students have to create both new "topics" and new "posts." A topic suggests a new thread for discussion, and often appears at the top of the screen online. A post is a written response to other posts within a topic. It's not complicated if you think of the forum as an outline. Here's a sample of how a forum might be organized:

First Screen: forum name *(example: English Class)*

Click on the forum name, and you're led to a new screen with several topics:

Second Screen: topics

(Othello—symbols)

(Othello—themes)

(Othello—characters)

Click on one of these topics, and you'll see any posts students have written:

Third Screen:

(Student post one: a discussion of the handkerchief as a symbol)

(Student post two: responding to student post one)

(Student post three: suggesting the color black as a symbol)

And so on. At any time, a student (or you) can jump between topics, add posts, or even add a new topic (your instructions should be clear about when this is allowed). On many forums, new topics can be added indefinitely, so that the outline shape of responses becomes more and more evident (this organizational screen works just like the folders and subfolders in which you keep documents on the drives of your computer).

- Because forums use this formal organization scheme, some preparation on the part of the teacher makes them much easier and more productive for students to use. Below are two examples of organizational strategies I often use.

Example One: Group Work

- Set up a new topic that identifies each of several groups in your class. These topics can just be named "group one," "group two," and so on, or they can more precisely identify the groups involved. My favorite use of this assignment is for outside reading or projects. I might, for instance, have different students in my class read different Shakespearean comedies (I might even let them choose which one they read, keeping in mind that choice often leads to greater interest and investment). Then each student could go to the forum and find a relevant topic—one for *All's Well That Ends Well,* one for *A Comedy of Errors,* and so on. Similarly, I might assign groups and give each an aspect of style to discuss about a passage; thus one topic might be called "similes and metaphors," another might be called "diction," and a third "sentence structure."

- Give each group a time limit (usually a number of days or class periods), a number of posts each member should submit for full credit, and some instructions about what you expect to see in the posted responses. Encourage students to actually respond to one another's ideas and points, not just to post unrelated points in order to get the assignment done (you might consider an overall discussion grade as well as a completion grade for number and timeliness of posts). My general rule of thumb: Students should be able to post about three substantial (one sentence to one paragraph each) responses for each class period or daily homework assignment; thus, if I give a class two evenings to complete the forum assignment, I'd expect around six posts from each student.

- If your students use screen names other than their full names for the posts, be sure to get a list of those screen names from them (screen names can offer students anonymity, which sometimes encourages discussion).

- At the end of the time period, read the posts and follow up as you would with any student discussion. Have the groups present, write a response of your own to the groups, have the class complete a writing assignment using the ideas and evidence provided by the posts, or use any other follow-up activity.

Example Two: A Class Discussion

- Rather than setting up a topic for each group, set up a number of topics for the whole class to discuss. Here's an approach that works well for preparing students to write the timed essay portion of an AP exam or the SAT: Make each new topic a sample essay question (the sample page included previously shows a series of responses to such an assignment on the novel *The God of Small Things*). I sometimes post as many as fifteen separate essay topics for a class to discuss.

- Instruct each student to post a certain number of responses on the forum within a period of days. Again, I usually require students to write about three substantial posts per day for two or three days (a class of twenty-five would thus post, collectively, seventy-five responses each day, or five responses per essay question if there are fifteen essay questions). In this case, responses should discuss possible answers to the question, possible evidence to support those answers, or questions or comments about the nature of the question or the answers.

- When the time limit is up, give each student a grade based on the number, length, and quality of responses.

- Instruct the students to read *all* of the posted responses by a certain time—a couple of days (you could also use class time for this activity, but I prefer this part of the assignment to remain homework).

- Choose any three of the fifteen or so essay topics. From these three, allow students to choose one and write a timed essay in response. Here's what this accomplishes:

  * Students have a chance to write an "on-demand" essay with some minimal preparation, but not total preparation. If they've done the work, they'll have considered—and discussed—all of the possible topics, but will not be able to write the complete essay in advance.

  * Students will need to read *all* of the posts in order to prepare adequately. If they read, say, only half of the posts, they might just miss all three of the questions you assign.

  * Students will feel the need, when posting the original responses, to spread their responses out among the possible prompts. I sometimes hint that I'm likely to choose the three set essay questions by looking at those with the least number of posted responses, though in fact I usually choose neither the most nor least popular prompts for the final essay.

Follow-up Ideas

My mother is a teacher in a different city from the one in which I live. A couple of years ago, we discovered that we were both teaching *A Tale of Two Cities* and *The God of Small Things* at roughly the same time. The beauty of the Internet here was apparent: Our students could discuss these novels with one another even though they live hundreds of miles apart and have class at different times.

Following the guidelines for the second assignment above, we posted a number of AP-style essay prompts about both books on a forum and had students from both schools post replies. The results were interesting. Students not only enjoyed the replies more, they admitted to trying a little harder to do the assignment well; their awareness that the audience for their thoughts had expanded raised their expectations of themselves even though the posts were, essentially, anonymous (each teacher knew the identities of the students, but the students at the different schools would most likely never meet one another, and were identified online only by screen names). At the end of a set period of time, each of us gave an essay test just as I've described above. Students at both schools rated the lesson very highly; in fact, a couple even got onto the forum *after* the test just to compare between schools. They wanted to see if both teachers had used the same three essay topics (we had).

Even if you can't find a teacher at another school (or in another city, state, or country) whose students can post along with yours, the principle holds firm: If you teach the same preparation multiple times, use a forum to have one class period communicate with another. You might also use a forum to have students from one teacher's class talk with those from another teacher's class. Broadening the audience may just enthuse your students to write a bit more carefully or just a bit more, and it may make the whole activity more fun.

Connecting to Current Events

Because a forum allows students the time to reflect and construct a careful response, it can be a good medium for discussions about issues that may seem controversial or delicate. I've used an online forum, for instance, after the topic of the deaths of loved ones came up in a creative writing class. Students had the option, though not the assignment, of posting their thoughts on a forum for continued discussion. Of course, I monitored the forum very closely and responded to students myself, as well.

There's a potential danger here, however—the same danger that one often finds in emailed communication: Because a written post does not convey tone or the subtleties of spoken language, it's easy for a less sophisticated writer to be sarcastic, attempt a joke, or unintentionally insult the reader. It's also easy for the reader to miss sarcasm. It's a worthwhile exercise to discuss online discourse with students in advance and to monitor forum postings about issues that may strike personal chords.

TECHNOLOGY EXERCISE 3: TRACKING CHANGES

Introduction

A main benefit of chat rooms, instant messaging, and an online forum is the opportunity technology affords to extend the classroom—to carry on a discussion or group project when not all of the participants are in the same physical space. As technology has become a routine part of the educational sphere, I've also searched for ways in which technology can offer sound classroom practice *and* benefit me as a teacher. In other words, I've tried to answer questions that always linger about technology and the classroom: Do computers really make our work more efficient? Does email lighten the paper load or just replace it?

Honestly, the first time I allowed a class of students to email me their written assignments with the idea that it would be "easier" for me, I wound up dismayed. There are some serious drawbacks to relying on online text, especially for teachers who love the written word for what it is: written. Email attachments are easy to forget about, take a long time to print out, and can be hard to manage if students don't format or title them correctly; electronic files turned in on a disk or CD aren't much better. There are still times when I regret allowing students to email me for all of these reasons, when I wind up printing out all of the pages when the authors could have done it for me.

But that's not the whole picture, and I'm not exaggerating when I say that discovering a few tricks about using technology for assessment and dialogue with students has revolutionized the way I grade and teach. A couple of simple but important realizations helped me get to this point.

1. I can type faster than I write by hand.

2. When I type, I often write more than I would by hand (this is true for students, as well).

3. When I type comments, I can return papers to students and also keep them myself.

As I said: simple but important. And, despite these truths, I still handwrite comments on papers frequently for many reasons—papers are easier to transport without a computer attached and handwriting does offer a personal touch.

When I want to comment extensively or in detail, however, I do it electronically, using some important features of my word-processing program: the ability to "track changes," the ability to highlight text (in color), and the ability to create text boxes within a document. The example of a graded document that follows, for instance, looks substantially different from those papers I grade by hand, which have minimal comments at the top and include any number of comments written sideways in margins as well as arrows and circles and abbreviations that may be intimidating and all but incomprehensible to students. (As you look at the example, keep in mind that on my computer and on the screen of the student, the highlighted area would appear in color.)

Tracking Changes: Sample Paper with Teacher Comments

Following are three sample introductory paragraphs by a twelfth-grade student, Nadia. Nadia wrote the essay in class and then, for homework, typed and emailed to me her introductory paragraph. The next day, after we spent the class period discussing strong introductions and sentence structure, I emailed my comments back to Nadia. She then rewrote the paragraph on her own. All three versions—the original, the original with my comments, and her revision—are included here.

Nadia's Original Paragraph:

Barry Unsworth's Morality Play is a sullen, plague-ridden tale of a traveling company of players who decide to investigate and reenact the murder of a small-town boy during the Middle Ages. Building on these themes, which appear throughout the novel, Unsworth strives to portray a world inundated with wickedness, yet not entirely barren of good. Unsworth depicts a time when these two conflicting powers co-exist, where death is merely an inevitability, and where all are simply players of the universe. As Nicholas Barber, the narrator, says, "The life of man upon earth is a warfare" (Unsworth 144).

Nadia's Paragraph with My Comments:

Nadia,

What a great start! You've managed to put together a solid thesis/argument with some very nice language—this introduction is good, and can become even better. Good job getting a quotation in there as we discussed in class (though see my note below about its placement).

I'd love to see you go back and use some of the sample sentence structures we went over in class here—you could really strengthen this paragraph with some sophisticated syntax (the practice sentences you wrote in class were fantastic).

Keep up this good work!

Barry Unsworth's Morality Play Don't forget to underline titles! is a sullen, plague-ridden tale of a traveling company of players who decide to investigate and reenact the murder of a small-town boy during the Middle Ages. Building on these themes which appear throughout the novel, 1) did you really need the phrase I deleted? 2) can you name these themes and link the period to Unsworth's portrayal of it more specifically? Unsworth strives to portray a world inundated with wickedness, yet not entirely barren of good. Unsworth depicts a time when these two conflicting powers co-exist, where death is merely an inevitability, and where all are simply players of the universe. The previous sentence (highlighted) is really your thesis—I think you should end with it. It's nicely phrased and sets up the organization of your essay well. As Nicholas Barber, the narrator, says, "The life of man upon earth is a warfare" (Unsworth 144). <u>Good quotation, but maybe you should move it up and end with the strong ideas of the previous sentence, your thesis. Isn't Nicholas quoting something here? Look it up . . . .</u>

Nadia's rewrite:

"The life of man upon earth is a warfare" (Unsworth 144), says Nicholas Barber, *Morality Play*'s twenty-three year old narrator, citing the book of *Job*. Barry Unsworth certainly meant for the essence of these words to resonate throughout his sullen, plague-ridden tale of a traveling company of players who decide to investigate and reenact the murder of a small-town boy during the Middle Ages. Death, corruption, and evil are evident themes which play integral, if not central roles, in the actions and message of the story itself. In such a dark and even morbid tale, Unsworth strives to portray a world inundated with wickedness, yet not entirely barren of good. It is with this idea of realism in mind that Unsworth depicts a time when these two conflicting powers co-exist, where death is merely an inevitability, where "God and the Devil are merely personages. God is a judge, Satan is an advocate" (56), and all are simply players of the universe.

Tracking Changes: Guidelines for Use

In this section, I list various tools that may be available to you in a word-processing program and ideas for using each to encourage students discussion both with other students and with the instructor.

Tracking Changes

- In Microsoft Word, the Track Changes option is available under the Tools menu or by simply pressing Ctrl+Shift+E on the keyboard. When you activate this function, all changes to the document appear in red. By choosing Options under the same menu, you can also determine other ways changes might be marked (underlined, different colors, or with notes about the change in the margins). The function can be deactivated at any time with the same keys, and there is also an Accept Changes function that formats the new data so that it looks like the rest of your text.

- When students track changes in peer editing, the result may come closer to written discussion than it does to simple proofreading. Certainly this is true of my own grading and editing. I am likely to write several times as much when I am typing directly into an essay as I am if I handwrite or even separately type comments. Tracked changes remain intact when emailed, so I have students comment on/edit each other's essays this way and email them both to the author and to me.

- In addition, more than one reader can track changes, and the new comments show up in a new color. Thus you can have several students comment on a single author's essay, story, poem, or article, and all of the individual comments can be identified—red for the first student, blue for the second, green for the third, and so on. Thus, actual discussion often takes place in the written comments to a piece, with each reader able to respond to the others as comments are added.

- The great benefit of this approach: When the student is ready to revise, all of the comments are embedded in a single document. Gone are the days of multiple photocopies with scratched corrections and comments on each. An author can accept one sentence automatically, revise another, and leave a third intact, all the while working in a single document. It's also hard to ignore comments at this point—they're in the text, so they must be dealt with in one way or another. Tracking changes can even allow a student to respond to those comments in the written work itself. The author can add comments in a new color and send it back to the reader. I've seen student papers in which, ultimately, the comments in various colors far outnumber the lines of original text; that's a not a bad thing when it comes to revision.

- I sometimes use track changes to write overall comments using a rubric. I set up the rubric in advance, then track changes to add individual comments for each student into the actual rubric. The student can then see the expectation and my assessment of how a specific paper meets that expectation, with a clear visual distinction between the two. I can also simply email the entire response to the student at once.

Highlighting Text

- Highlighting is most easily accomplished by using the icon on the Formatting toolbar in Microsoft Word. The process is easy: Select a word, phrase, or chunk of text, click on the highlight icon, and the text is highlighted in the color of your choice.

- I sometimes use this function when commenting or editing student work. I might highlight a section of text and then track changes; in my comments, I refer to the "green text" or the "yellow text" so the student can correlate my comment to the original text. I've also used this function to point out, for instance, the overuse of a single word by highlighting the word each time it appears—a stark visual that, again, the student must deal with, because it's there in the document.

- In order to provoke discussion about writing, I start each year by having students highlight certain elements in the first essay they write. The first night, for homework, they must highlight every single verb in the essay. The next day in class I ask certain students to read just the verbs from their essays, then we discuss the value of interesting verbs and the difficulties that arise for the reader when the verb *to be* appears in eighteen consecutive sentences. The second night, I might have students highlight (in a new color) the first four words of every sentence, and the next class might include a discussion of sentence variety. We can go on indefinitely, highlighting in various colors adjectives, adverbs, punctuation, polysyllabic words, transition words, compound sentences, quoted evidence, and any other aspect of the essay that's worth paying particular attention to. Eventually, a revision takes into account all of these individual elements and tries to improve the overall quality of the essay. Could you do with this with an ink highlighter and a printed essay? Sure. But the process would be tedious and the revision even more so.

Text Boxes

> This is an example of a text box.

- A text box is exactly what it sounds like—a box with text in it. What's nice about text boxes (which are easiest to insert using an icon on the Drawing toolbar in Word) is that they can be inserted absolutely anywhere—in margins, over existing text, and in other places (like the space next to the subheading above) where you might not type otherwise. They can also be moved around the page, text intact, at any time without disrupting other text, and they can easily be reduced or enlarged to include more or fewer words.

- Text boxes, like tracked changes, are useful for commenting on a written piece. The difference: Tracking changes allows for quick, extensive comments or insertions, and the information can then be easily included in the original document. A text box stands out.

- Text boxes are especially useful for exchanging comments and discussion about works in which formatting is important, such as poetry. Students can comment on their own decisions in original poems or peer edit and discuss each other's poetry without changing the line breaks or structure of the original poem. Text boxes can be used with prose, as well; sometimes an emphatic comment about a whole paragraph, for instance, can best be made by using a text box.

- Another discussion possibility: When studying poetry, have students complete group discussion by exchanging electronic versions of the poem with text boxes. You might, for instance, assign each student in a pair a Shakespearean sonnet. Using one text box per quatrain and one for the couplet (four in all), have each student paraphrase the poem and send it to his or her partner. Then have the students respond to the paraphrases (the exchange can go back and forth as long as it's productive) and exchange documents again. The original poem remains intact, but the student discussion builds in the margins.

Other Word-Processing Tools That Promote Reflection and Discussion

- There's an interesting feature of Word under the Tools menu called Autosummarize. The program will automatically highlight those sentences or points in a piece of writing that its electronic brain decides are important. The value I find in this function is its ability to promote discussion. Students can use the feature on an original essay or a short story by an author, then discuss how well the program makes decisions about which important points or topic sentences to isolate. By extension, classes end up discussing not only what the key points of a specific written work are, but also how we identify and read for key points and ideas in general.

- Inserting "hyperlinks" (a function located under the Insert menu) allows students to create a link between two words or sentences—click on one, and the screen jumps to the other. Combined with text boxes, this offers the chance to make connections between parts of a work or even between separate documents. For instance, a student might take two poems that share certain words, hyperlink between the words, and use text boxes to explain the relationship. Another student might then try out the links and read the explanations, leading ultimately to a discussion between students about other possible links or the overall thematic connection of the works.

- Most word-processing programs allow users to split the screen and view two documents at once. This can be useful in revision (students must retype a document while viewing the original) or in comparison (students can look at two poems or paragraphs at once on the same screen).

- Word-processing programs are a useful tool for brainstorming lists and compiling group data because lists can be easily saved, combined, emailed to other groups, edited, or projected for all to see.

Follow-up Ideas

One of the great advantages technology offers is the opportunity to equip students with tools for self-assessment. Assessment for educational purposes usually includes two steps: Step one involves judging the quality, quantity, and/or effort that student work represents, and step two involves quantifying that information, which is often arrived at subjectively or holistically, by assigning it a particular grade. The process often seems entirely subjective to students, who may not see past the final mark even when presented with comments, a rubric, or other means of explanation. I've handed back essays with paragraphs of my own comments attached only to have students turn to the last page, glance at the grade, and throw the whole thing into the trash. How, I ask myself, do I bridge the gap in a process in which I find the first step to be most important and the second, the actual grading, a bothersome necessity, and in which they see only the end result as meaningful?

Self-assessment takes—as do so many meaningful student activities—more time. It's just plain easier, and often more accurate, for a teacher to judge the quality of a paper. But self-assessment demands real reflection and learning from students; it also promotes a better understanding of the grading process that may pay off on later assignments when the teacher takes on the entire burden of grading. Of course, it's not enough just to ask students to decide their own grades subjectively. Rubrics help, but even with a detailed rubric, a student may skim over or ignore aspects of the work.

Technology helps. Most of my rubrics for written student work identify a percentage of the final grade that is assigned to quality of writing, quality of content or argumentation, and formatting (citation format, appropriate formatting of titles, and so on). Here are the sorts of categories that might appear on a typical rubric for grading an essay.

1. Content and argumentation: Does the essay make a strong argument, answer the question, relate the discussion to overall meaning, and present original ideas? Are quotations appropriate and well integrated? Is evidence from throughout the

novel included? Is the quotation clearly related to a major theme of the novel?

2. Quality of writing: Is the writing clear, stylistically interesting, without awkwardness and errors of syntax? Does sentence structure vary?

3. Organization: Is the paper well organized, with clear transitions, a logical flow, and a thorough introduction and conclusion?

4. Mechanical errors: Are usage and grammar correct? Are there specific errors that appear once or more in the paper?

One might get even more specific, for instance, by listing certain mechanical areas for assessment—focusing on comma use, formatting of quoted material, or sentence completion, for example.

When students self-assess using technology, I also ask them to review the overall process. Because it is so easy (and tidy) for students to keep multiple drafts, the process is often more transparent than with handwritten work. Here are the kinds of questions I might ask students to consider while reviewing their work online:

- Review your rough draft(s) and your final draft (with all changes tracked). Approximately what percentage of the paper underwent revision? How much of that revision was substantial and structural and how much was minor?

- In the final draft, highlight any sentence (line, paragraph) that you think is particularly effective. Highlight (in a new color) any sentence you think might be weak. Then, for each, use a textbox in the margin to explain your choice.

- In the rubric for this assignment, track changes and type a response to each item discussing how well you accomplished that part of the assignment.

Or, for a more detailed rubric that includes specific items, such as elements of grammar:

- Create a hyperlink from the rubric to your final document (or cut and paste from the document into the rubric) that takes the reader to a spot in your paper where you use each item correctly.

This sort of self-assessment doesn't necessarily lead to a student assigning his or her own work an accurate grade any more than any other form of reflection. It does, however, increase the chance for meaningful discussion about grades and quality of work between teachers and students, whether that discussion takes place orally or in, say, an email. The benefit here is that computers make the process engaging, organized, and visual and that some students may well say far more about their own work in this format than they would in a one-on-one, on-the-spot discussion with a teacher or with peers.

And don't forget, technology is fun for many students. A class period spent on a computer, even to work on writing, may engage some students who might otherwise tune out. In the end, some of the hassles—the difficulty of scheduling lab time, of managing email files from students, of dealing with the inevitable glitches and technical problems—may be worth the outcome as a class focuses on process, not just product.

Connecting to Current Events

Because a document with tracked changes can serve as a color-coded exchange of ideas within a single page (students don't even have to email one another; they can simply share a computer and keep tracking changes back and forth), this function of word processing is a great way to hold a written minidebate on current issues. The procedure I use for this method is simple.

First, I assign a yes/no question (relevant to our unit of study) to the class: "Is government-sanctioned torture acceptable when national security is at stake?" and "Should the United States seek to strengthen its ties with the United Nations or distance itself from that organization?" are recent examples from my own teaching.

Then, I put students in pairs and have each pair assign one person to answer "yes" and one to answer "no." The students write their answers into a single document, tracking changes each time a new student speaks. They are also allowed to hyperlink to relevant online sources as evidence of their points or to highlight the text of the debate in order to isolate and refute certain points.

When the period is over, I can view—and grade—a single document for each pair of students and can easily distinguish between the two authors. Of course, this technique can be used with literature, as well. A question such as "Was Hamlet, ultimately, more to blame for the deaths of Ophelia, Polonius, Gertrude, and Laertes than Claudius was?" can provoke the same sort of discussion and research online.

TECHNOLOGY EXERCISE 4: A THOUSAND WORDS

Introduction

As a lover of literature, I've always irrationally and, perhaps, indefensibly resented the old adage that tells us "a picture's worth a thousand words." I often want to rewrite the statement—a thousand words, I want to believe, are sometimes worth far more than a picture (otherwise, why is the book so often better than the movie?). But the truth is that every medium can inform us, stimulate the imagination, ask us to reexamine the world.

Cameras, tape recorders, and even video cameras have been around long enough to become standard tools available to teachers. Even the abilities to burn a CD, record a voice on a computer, or project a picture from a laptop onto a screen have existed for as long as many students can remember. What's new to many of us, as teachers, is the ease with which such information can be transported and used in the classroom. I can now snap a picture and, within a minute or two, have it projected on the wall for all to see. I can record a student performance and email it to everyone in the class. I can easily file away digital photographs of student work or presentations and find them a year later on a moment's notice.

The ideas included in this section are intended to help maximize this use of technology in order to promote discussion and communication in and between your classes. They're also a good way to ease technology use into your teaching—even if there's no love lost between you and those hulking desktop PCs in the computer lab. The technology included here is cheap, easy to use, and immediately gratifying (and it rarely requires calling in a team of I.T. experts to figure out why you hooked everything up wrong and can't get things to work).

Sample Activity: A Thousand Words

For years, I've made an assignment that required groups of students to assemble original photographs to represent each line of a short poem, such as cummings' "since feeling is first," Williams' "The Red Wheelbarrow," or Wordsworth's "My Heart Leaps Up." Once, I'd even pay to develop the film, but those days are gone. Now I have students take the photographs using a digital camera, assemble the pictures in Powerpoint, and email the file to me. I've also—and this is perhaps less creative but much easier—just had students gather photos from the Internet (with proper citation of sources, of course) for their projects. I've also allowed artistic students to create some of their illustrations with computer art programs, and I've even had students use video as part of the project.

On the surface, the results aren't so different: What used to come to me as a poster with photos messily taped to it and handwritten lines of poetry underneath now arrives through cyberspace as a program with photos inserted and typed lines from the poems.

What's changed is the next step. With small prints, I'd just tape the posters on the wall—even passing them around was unwieldy and too often resulted in the photographs falling off the posters. Now I take a different approach:

- After all of the PowerPoint documents have been emailed to me, I email all of the documents back to the whole class. However, these files can be big; an alternative is to project them onto a screen and view the PowerPoints as a class before moving on to the next step.

- We discuss each poem and the photos that accompany it while the creators of the project remain silent. Where a connection seems tenuous or abstract, we try as a class to decide what connection the author of the project saw between the visual image and the written words. Only when this discussion concludes may the creator of the project explain his or her intent.

- Next comes the fun part: "If a picture is worth a thousand words," I say to the class, "surely a poem and a bunch of pictures are worth at least that much. Your job now is to choose any one of these poems and answer the questions I'm about to give you in a written paper." The questions are these:

  * How does the visual imagery of the poem reinforce its overall meaning?

  * Having seen all of the projects, what images and connections in this presentation do you think work best? What other pictures or images might you use to illustrate the meaning of the poem?

  * Is the poem relevant to today's world, and if so, how?

  Then I add the kicker: "By the way, when I said a thousand words, I meant it. You must answer in exactly one thousand words—no more, no less."

One thousand words is actually quite a bit for many high school students, but I also find that the complex connections between image and poetry offer many students so much to write about that they come back complaining about having to cut text in order to stay within the limit. An alternative, if you worry about the length of the assignment, might be to have a group of students write about a single poem, taking one question each, with the restriction that altogether, their responses must equal exactly one thousand words.

A Thousand Words: Guidelines for Use

There are many ways to use tape recorders, digital cameras, and video cameras in the classroom to record and share student performances, group projects, and memorable moments. I keep a digital camera handy at all times simply to capture such moments—not just so that the class can watch later, but also so that other classes might watch. Such technology isn't only useful for recording events, however; it's also a good way to spark discussion. Here are a few ideas about how to generate more thought and dialogue in your classes using cameras and recorders.

- Take pictures of projects in one class and share them with other classes. This is especially useful if you teach multiple sections of the same course. Ask students to discuss the work other classes are doing. This can promote both a sense of connection to other classes and, sometimes, a healthy sense of competition (I don't encourage this *too* much, but when students know their work will be shared with other classes, it sometimes prompts them to put in a bit more effort).

- Allow students to use cameras and recorders to prepare short presentations before class begins, then share them in class. One friend of mine has one student assigned each day to share a "poem of the day"—the twist is that instead of just reading the poem aloud to a class, the student tape records the reading and it's shared with all of the teacher's classes that day. Some students even add digital photos or video to their readings. As a result of the performance aspect, students generally prepare their readings more thoroughly, and the resulting discussions of the poems often mirror the increased interest of the audience.

- Use a video camera to generate discussion or discussion groups across classes. A simple way to do this is to pose a question to all of your students and then film a few from each class answering. The next day, play all of the responses for all of your classes and use the results as a discussion-starter. The benefit here is that the students hear some points of view other than those of class members; I often try this approach if I feel that we've more or less exhausted the diversity of viewpoints in a single class or section of a course.

- Use a digital camera to connect imagery to texts. It's amazing how much discussion a single image can generate, especially if there's a connection to words that's not completely literal. I recall, for instance, a question from a student in one class about why Jane Austen so often includes sisters as main characters.

The next day I found three or four pairs of students at our school who were sisters and took their pictures. Then I showed those pictures to the class and asked for responses. The resulting discussion explored some interesting questions of psychology, the differences between childhood relationships and adult relationships, and the importance of family in the historical context of Austen's novels.

Follow-up Ideas

One of the most exciting aspects of technology such as digital cameras and the ability to record sound on computers is how easy it becomes to capture and share what happens in your classroom. Most often, I simply wish to share these moments later on with the students involved. Consider, though, other ways of sharing such material.

- Show students what's happening in other classes.
- Show students projects and presentations from previous years to current classes.
- Email parents pictures of events in your classroom. This is a great way to share memorable events without writing lengthy letters, and parents love the visual access. You can also collect images and recordings in a PowerPoint or other program to share on parent information nights and at special events.
- Email administrators pictures of events in your classroom. Often, no message is required—it can simply be refreshing for an administrator to feel that connection to good work students are completing.
- Save pictures and recordings to show to the class later in the year; a visual reminder of earlier lessons can be a great way to connect new texts to the themes and activities you've done in the past.

Connecting to Current Events

Some of the above activities are easily adaptable to the study of current events. For instance, in some social studies classes, I've instituted a regular "news story of the day" instead of a "poem of the day." Some students even chose to videotape their news reports beforehand and "air" them as a daily news show.

Digital photos can also be used to document student reports, projects, and discussions revolving around social and political issues. Try, for instance, taking some pictures of the school cafeteria before discussing racial issues in schools with your students. Have students segregated themselves or not? Why? Similarly, pictures of how boys and girls sit in various classrooms might provoke some discussion of gender issues and how gender is treated by schools. Because schools frequently function as a microcosm of society, many good discussions of such issues can begin with a discussion of how the issue plays out in the school environment, and a visual image to accompany such discussion can raise new questions and insights.

6 *Formal Discussion and Debate*

DEBATE EXERCISE 1: DEBATE

Introduction

Students—and teachers—often use the terms *discussion* and *debate* interchangeably, but I think of these two forms of communication as distinct from one another. Although the format of each may look similar, and though discussion may sometimes become debate, the purpose of a discussion, as I think of it, is different from that of a debate. A discussion promotes thinking about all sides of an issue; a debate attempts to prove that just one side is correct. In a discussion, there are no winners or losers; debate attempts to produce both a winner and a loser. In a discussion, questions can stand without definitive answers; in a debate, the best answers are valued.

There's a place for debate in the classroom, but as rule, I prefer discussion for most activities. I prefer to leave students working out answers on their own; I prefer not to have winners and losers both because the winner of a debate may be less correct or accurate than vocal and eloquent and because some students focus more on winning than on learning. I also, for the most part, like to find ways for quieter students to express themselves.

Nonetheless, a structured, carefully planned debate may be the perfect tool for exploring some topics. Debate does, of course, emphasize public speaking skills, but that's not all: debate activities generally illuminate the importance of research, preparation, organization of an argument, teamwork, and summarization. Debates also offer the opportunity for students to take on multiple roles, from speaker to moderator to audience; they can also provide powerful connections to important contemporary and historical issues, as debate has been the classic model of political discourse for centuries.

Many schools, of course, operate forensics programs, and information is readily available on the Internet for those interested in competitions between school teams. The activities included in this section are meant, rather, for classroom use, and so may be amended or adjusted to suit the topic, class, or purpose of the assignment.

Sample Activity: Debate

I prefer to phrase formal debate topics as questions so that there is a clear goal for student arguments. In one recent class, I posed the following topics to a class as we completed our study of *1984*.

- Is the use of torture justified when national interests are at stake?
- Is it worth giving up some civil liberties in order to guarantee the safety of the majority of citizens?
- Must a nation have a single strong leader in order to maintain its strength as a nation?
- If a government controls mass media and print resources, can it control the thoughts of its citizens?
- Can a single citizen make a difference in the way a national government operates?

My choice of these statements was intentional; each is derived from events in the novel, from the torture of Winston Smith in room 101 to his work at the Ministry of Information, but each also reflects an important issue that faces our society today. In fact, I've since seen editorials in my local newspaper that take a side on every one of these issues.

It didn't take the students long to pick up on the connection. As soon as I finished writing the questions on the board, one student, Chris, raised his hand.

"Is the second question referring to the Patriot Act?" he asked.

I shrugged. "Does the Patriot Act require you to give up civil liberties?" I responded.

"Sure."

"OK," I said. "Which ones?"

Chris grimaced. "Well, I'm not sure exactly which ones, but I know there's something about searching your house in there."

"Yeah," agreed Rebecca, another student in the class. "It says something about legal representation for terrorist suspects too, doesn't it?"

There was no doubt, at the moment, that the questions I posed would have formed the basis for a lively discussion. At the same time, though, I could tell that the discussion would include some misinformation and assumptions, and the points the students were raising were too important to their understanding of our own government, much less the one in the book, to ignore. A formal debate, in this case, seemed not only a useful method but a necessary one.

I broke students into groups, gave each one a question, and required research into the subject as homework. We discussed how this research might be conducted, including the need for the students to judge the reliability and bias of their sources. Step one, for Chris and Rebecca, was looking up the text of the Patriot Act, as well as criticism and defense of its provisions from reliable writers and speakers.

The resulting debates—five in all—took three days of class and included every student in the class. In the end, however, the time was worth it. Did the students gain a better understanding of the ideas presented in *1984*? Probably. More importantly, they gained both a better understanding of our own society and government and a greater sense of connection to a piece of literature. That's the elusive goal I'm always striving for, that connection, and because it lasts so much longer than the results of most lessons I teach, it's worth a couple of extra days of class to get it.

Debate: Guidelines for Use

There's a classic form of debate that's been used in more or less similar fashion at least since Lincoln and Douglas squared off against one another over slavery in 1859, and it still works. In this form, each of several students receives a role, generally including:

- affirmative position debaters
- negative position debaters
- responders and rebutters for both affirmative and negative teams
- moderators (who introduce debaters, pose questions or topics, and set agenda)
- summarizers

A typical debate in this format might run something like the actual structure used by Lincoln and Douglas.

- One student presents the affirmative positions on the question.
- The second student asks questions, challenging the affirmative points.

- The second student then presents the negative positions.
- The first student asks questions, challenging the negative points.
- The first student offers a general rebuttal of the negative position.
- The second student offers a general rebuttal of the positive position.
- The first student offers a second, shorter rebuttal of the negative position.

Times may be assigned to each part of this process, and the rest of the class can serve as moderators, judges, questioners, or simply as audience members. The format works, but it's time-consuming and limits participation mainly to two (or at least very few) students.

For this reason, I often use other, simpler formal debate formats. Try this, for instance:

- Divide students into odd-numbered groups (I prefer groups of five). Present each group with one question (such as those outlined in the sample activity above).
- Allow the groups to assign roles according to the following guidelines.
  - * Each group must have two people to argue the "yes" side of the argument.
  - * Each group must have two people to argue the "no" side of the argument.
  - * Each group must have one person to summarize the argument and take the lead in answering questions.
- Give the groups time to research the topic. Require each group to find a reasonable number (I usually require three) of reliable sources that address the topic.
- Once the groups have researched, have them discuss the topic as a group, constructing *both* positive and negative arguments.
- Have each group present the argument to the class in the following format:
  - * One student presents a positive argument. (I usually limit speaking time to one minute per student. This not only keeps things moving but makes preparation that much more important.)
  - * Another student presents a negative argument and/or rebuts the positive points.
  - * The third student presents more positive arguments and/or rebuts negative points.

> * The fourth student presents more negative arguments and/or rebuts other points.
>
> * The fifth student, who may take notes as the previous four speaks, summarizes the arguments from both sides.

- When the group is finished presenting, it takes questions from the class. The summarizer should choose who asks each question and may also direct certain questions to certain members of the group. (At this point, the teacher may wish to ask questions as well, but be careful not to argue a point; rather, play devil's advocate and allow the students to respond.)

- When the debate is finished, ask the members of the group what they really feel about the issue. Did they argue from their own viewpoints or did they simply argue a point? Allow the class to discuss—or possibly even vote on—their general feeling about the question.

Follow-up Ideas

Because a successful debater may well leave his or her opponent stumped, debates sometimes seem one-sided and a class may feel sure that one "answer" to the question being scrutinized is clear. It's therefore quite important that some follow-up activity, whether it takes the form of informal discussion or written response, encourages each student in the class to reflect upon the topic, the arguments that have been presented by the debaters, and his or her own position.

One of my own high school teachers made an assignment I've never forgotten that forced me to think through both sides of an issue. While we were studying *Antigone*, Mr. Kaplan assigned us each to write a two-page defense of Antigone's actions in the play. Then, the next night, our homework was to write a similar defense of Creon's actions. Simple as it was, the assignment drove home a powerful point: When you force yourself to think as a supporter of a position, you understand the position better, and often become attached to it; forcing yourself then to change sides balances your viewpoint and deepens your overall understanding of the topic. I've since used this approach as a follow-up to formal debates in the classroom, asking students to write a defense of both positions before choosing one to support.

Connecting to Current Events

In addition to completing written assignments, students need to reflect on the potential drawbacks and benefits of a polarized argument by thinking about how debate functions in our own society—the kind of forum in which one might find such polarity and the rhetoric it encourages. Three activities follow that draw upon the schisms in opinion encouraged by formal debate and that require some thought about current issues.

- Use an oral debate as a springboard for studying editorials and writing letters to the editor for your school or local newspaper. The editorial page of many newspapers is a common forum for both partisan arguments and ongoing debate in the community. Give your students a sample editorial page and discuss tactics, rhetorical strategies, flaws in argumentation, constraints placed upon the writing by the medium in which it appears, and possible responses to arguments presented in the written pieces. Then have students write their own letters or editorials on a subject of importance to the students and the community. You may wish actually to submit the best of these for publication, but it's not necessary for the point to get across.

- Watch or read a transcript from an actual political debate, one from your community or one of national importance. Ask your class to point out the differences between debate and discussion and to judge the merits of the arguments (and the questions asked by the moderator). You might then reenact the debate in your class (you could also do this before viewing the actual debate) by posing the same questions to student debaters; you might also follow up with a written assignment or small-group discussions that allow students the chance to respond to or summarize the arguments made by both sides in the debate.

- Effective oral speech often relies heavily on rhetorical strategies and devices—parallel structure and syntactical series, for instance, become important means of not only communicating ideas but making those ideas memorable and adding emotional gravity to them. Review the texts of some historical speeches with your students; you might use a famous presidential address, the addresses of authors such as William Faulkner or Toni Morrison upon accepting the Nobel prize for literature, or other historical speeches. Have your class pick out effective (or ineffective) examples of rhetoric from the speeches for discussion. It's also interesting to compare the rhetoric of such discourse to that of fictional speeches delivered by characters such as, for instance, Marc Antony or Atticus Finch.

DEBATE EXERCISE 2: RULES OF ORDER

Introduction

Several years ago, I saw a Model United Nations (MUN) simulation for the first time. Unfortunately, the particular MUN session I observed was a disaster. The students were unruly and the "chair" of the session, another student, seemed to have little or no control over the situation. At the same time, I could appreciate the structure and possibilities for discussion that such parliamentary simulations offer; years later, I've not only observed, sponsored, and chaired MUN sessions myself, I use the simulation as a regular activity in social studies classes.

But MUN—and programs like it such as Model Congress—is complicated and time-consuming; what follows is *not* a description of how to run such simulations. Rather, this exercise is designed to help teachers take advantage of the excellent possibilities that the parliamentary debate structure can offer.

Here's what I saw, even in that first session (and have seen work wonderfully many other times), as the main aspects of the program:

- role-playing (in the sense of representing a particular point of view—no heavy acting required)
- the use of documents as a focal point for debating complicated issues
- strict rules and structures for debate (parliamentary procedure)

For most teachers unfamiliar with parliamentary procedures, the last item on this list probably seems most intimidating; it can seem that way for students, as well.

What I offer here is a simplified version of the rules of order used in MUN and similar simulations. Keep in mind that there is still a learning curve involved, both for teacher and student. Using parliamentary procedure in any form is more complicated than most discussion methods. The benefits of this structure, though, are several.

- This structure encourages many, if not all, students to speak—including normally quiet or reserved students.
- It ensures civility for complex and controversial subjects.
- When used appropriately, many students find it quite fun.
- It encourages attention to formal and informal speech and rhetoric.
- It allows complicated issues to be broken down carefully and systematically for analysis, debate, and evaluation.
- It makes the role-playing aspect of the exercise far less threatening.

Used well, this activity will not result in the sort of failed exercise I witnessed at that first MUN. On the contrary, it instills a higher sense of order and discipline into a discussion than I might achieve otherwise (I've even used this activity when I'm being observed or evaluated by administrators). What's more, I've never once had a class complain that we were using this procedure too much; most of my students enjoy it so much, in fact, that they want to participate in such debate on a regular basis.

Rules of Order: Sample Scenarios

In preparing an activity using the parliamentary structure, I ask myself two questions.

- What particular points of view, if any, do I want represented in the debate?
- What do I want the final product (almost always a written document) to look like?

Here are some examples that I've used successfully:

Possible Roles for Students	Possible Documents (Product)
• *characters from texts*	
pilgrims from *The Canterbury Tales*	a declaration of the "best" tale
rulers of note in literature	a list of principles for monarchs
Greek gods and goddesses	a declaration of the rights of humans
• *authors*	
representatives of various literary movements	a definition of literature of merit
poets of the seventeenth century	guidelines for writing love poems
female authors of various periods	guidelines for choosing a good subject for a novel
• *critics*	
editors of a journal or anthology	the best three poems by one poet (e.g., for inclusion in an anthology)
representatives of schools of critical theory	guidelines for reading a text
• *no particular roles*	any of the above, or:
(students debate from their own points of view)	a list of the best 10 books ever written
	a definition of poetry, drama, etc.
	a list of classroom rules
	the best possible introductory paragraph (for an essay or story)

Quite often, I opt not to assign students to particular roles—though if a class tends to come to consensus easily, it's a good way to ensure a variety of opinions in the debate. It's important to note, however, that this isn't meant to be primarily an acting exercise. The idea is not so much to have a student, say, act like Jane Austen or Elizabeth Bennet as it is to have the student debate by making the points Austen or Bennet might—the ideas and substance, not the style or appearance.

The list of possible products is nearly endless, and all of the above can be adapted or even traded with one another fairly readily. The point is to find a type of document students can create both on their own and as a class—one that will serve well as a final product at the end of the exercise.

Rules of Order: Guidelines for Use

At the heart of any good activity that uses parliamentary procedure is the adherence to rules that no one—neither teacher nor student—may consider violable. It's this idea of a structure that binds everyone that makes many students enjoy the exercise, because it makes the process transparent without determining the end product.

The importance of rules also means that the most important position is that of the chair, even though the chair takes no substantive role in the discussion itself. I usually serve as chair myself in classroom activities until everyone in the room is comfortable enough with the procedure for a student to take over, at which point I become a participant (if you have no students with experience in the procedure, it can take days for the class to reach this comfort level).

A sample order of debate is included after these guidelines. Of course, this order may be altered in many ways. Here are some overall guidelines for combining this order of debate with the sample scenarios.

- Assign each student a role and have him or her create, if appropriate, documents for discussion (see the previous scenarios for some suggestions). In some cases, you may wish to pair students in a role, but I recommend limiting each role to two students so that more students are encouraged to speak. The documents students create should all be in the same form.

- Decide in advance, by yourself or with the help of students, the order of debate and rules.

- Photocopy all of the sample documents and give each student a copy of every paper. Label the documents by letter or number for easy reference.

- Formally call the session to order (a gavel to pound on a podium is a nice touch here).
- Follow the order of debate carefully, calling on students at the appropriate times and keeping careful track of time and procedure.
- Continue debate until the goal (a single document, a list, a selection of three poems, for example) has been reached.
- Formally adjourn the session.

Once a consensus (or majority vote) has been reached and the class has a final product, end the formal debate and discuss the process and its results. Among the questions you might ask students to consider:

- How well did you stay in character? Was it harder or easier than you expected?
- How do you feel about the final product? Is it the best possible product or merely a good compromise?
- What frustrated you about the debate format or content? What worked well?

Rules of Order: Sample Order of Debate

In an effort to create a simple structure for debate that takes just one class period, I simplify and abbreviate the debate order and rules used in many formal simulations. First of all, I stipulate the following conditions.

- All votes require only a simple majority to pass.
- All votes are simple placard votes. Each student makes a placard with his or her role identified on it and, during a vote, holds the placard up silently to signify a yes or no vote.
- All speakers have exactly one minute in which to speak.
- The following points of order—and only these—are acceptable (students call out one of these points to get the chair's attention, at which point the chair may interrupt the speaker long enough to clear up the point).
  * point of order (the chair or a student has not followed procedure correctly)
  * point of personal privilege (the student cannot hear, does not have a copy of a document, and so on)
  * point of information (the student needs to ask the chair a question)

These rules may be modified, of course. You might wish to allow longer or shorter speaker times, to take a roll call vote at the conclusion of a discussion, or to require a two-thirds majority for a vote. In a real parliamentary simulation, there are many more points, some of which may be used to interrupt the speaker and others only at appropriate times. As students become more familiar with the procedure, such modifications also become easier to implement.

Here, then, is the simplified order of debate I generally use.

- The chair calls the session to order.
- A student participant (recognized by the chair) moves to bring a document or topic to the floor. The motion is accepted if it is seconded.
  * The participant with whom the motion originates has one minute to speak "pro"—in favor of discussing the topic or document. The chair may recognize another participant to speak "con."
  * A vote is taken to determine whether or not the motion passes (if the motion fails, repeat the previous two steps).
- Once a document is on the floor:
  * The author of the document speaks in favor of it.
  * To start off the debate, the chair asks for one pro and one con speaker on the document itself. First, the con speaker is allowed the floor, then the pro speaker. Debate continues from this point with the chair calling alternately on con and pro speakers.
  * An alternative to the above step: The chair may take a "speaker's list" at the beginning of the debate and call on those on the list in order. This is a more formal procedure but can be rewarding, as it allows all to see the order of speakers and to prepare accordingly.
  * Debate continues uninterrupted unless or until one of the following happens.
    - A student calls out a point of order, privilege, or information
    - An amendment to the document being debated is submitted in writing to the chair. If the author submits this amendment, it becomes part of the document automatically when the chair acknowledges it. If another student submits the amendment, the chair may take speakers on the amendment and hold a vote

on whether or not to include/exclude the stipulated text. (*A note on amendments:* This part of the process is important because it allows students not only to revise documents but also to combine elements of various documents together. This can save time and result in a more satisfying final product for everyone.)

- The time limit for general debate comes to an end or a student moves to close debate, the motion is seconded, and the assembly votes in favor.

- General debate ends. The chair calls for voting procedures.

  * The author makes a closing statement.
  * Any final points are considered.
  * The assembly votes to accept or reject the document.

- If necessary, the chair accepts motions for a new document or topic to be brought to the floor and repeats the process.

Rules of Order: Sample Classroom Exchange

In a parliamentary debate, the tone set by the chair often determines the tone of the entire activity. Here's a sample transcript of a debate. In this example, the class is debating a definition of tragedy in literature and is focusing upon a sample document written by a student named Tim. You'll notice the concept of "yielding time" being used here when a speaker finishes.

CHAIR: Next on the speaker's list is Jennifer. Jennifer, you have the floor for one minute.

JENNIFER: I'd just like to point out that I agree with everything in this definition except for line seven, which suggests that a tragic hero has to die in order for a work to be classified as tragedy. I'm not sure death is necessary—maybe just a fall from power or something. I yield my time to the chair.

CHAIR: Thank you. Next on the speaker's list is Carlos. Carlos, you have the floor for one minute.

CARLOS: I agree with Jennifer, I think, but I'd like to hear what Tim has to say about it. Can I yield my time to Tim?

CHAIR: Yes. Tim, there are forty seconds left. You have the floor.

TIM: The problem with just saying a hero has to fall from power is that it's a gray area. Lots of characters fall from power. All of the great tragedies end with someone dying. Look at all of those Shakespeare plays.

JENNIFER: But what about—

CHAIR: I'm sorry, Jennifer, you're not in order. Tim still has the floor. Would you like to be added to the speaker's list again?

JENNIFER: Yes.

CHAIR: OK. Tim, do you wish to continue?

TIM: No, I yield my time to the chair.

SANDRA: Point of information!

CHAIR: Sandra, you're recognized.

SANDRA: May I be added to the speaker's list as well?

CHAIR: Yes. Are there any other points or motions? No? In that case, we return to the speaker's list. Mark has the floor for one minute.

MARK: Blanche DuBois didn't die in *Streetcar*. She just went nuts. That was pretty tragic.

CHAIR (after a pause): Mark, do you yield the rest of your time?

MARK: Yeah, sorry. I yield to, um, Jennifer.

JENNIFER: Hey everyone, I'm working on an amendment to re-place line seven in Tim's definition with lines three and four from Sandra's. It will be ready in a minute. Just keep talking until I can get this to the chair, please. If we make this change, I'll support this definition and vote for it, but if we don't, I'd rather move on to another definition and see if we can—

CHAIR: I'm sorry, your time has expired. Are there any points or motions?

TIM: I move for a three minute recess so we can talk about this amendment.

CHAIR: That motion is in order. Are there seconds? (Several hands are raised.) Very well, we'll vote on the motion for a brief re-cess of three minutes for the purpose of discussing a possible amendment. All in favor raise your placards now . . .

Follow-up Ideas

The parliamentary process is so exhaustive, frankly, that I don't always feel the need to follow up the exercise. Students have already debated, written, and arrived at a product by the end of the activity. A few questions for debriefing is often enough to give a sense of closure to such a discussion.

However, the product at which students arrive is rarely satisfactory to everyone; most often, it's the result of compromise, not consensus. Sometimes it's possible to compare such a product with one that already exists. Take, for instance, some of the sample scenarios presented earlier.

- A definition of tragedy might be compared to Aristotle's definition in *Poetics.*

- A declaration of the rights of humans (made by Greek mythological figures) might be compared to the United Nations Declaration of Human Rights.

- After agreeing on the three best poems by Emily Dickinson, the class might consult a text like the *Norton Anthology of Poetry* to see which poems are, in fact, included. (In this scenario, I'd assign each student one poem and have him or her construct a defense for it before the activity begins.)

You can, of course, use other follow-up techniques that have already been discussed—have students reflect in writing on the process, have them write from other points of view, or have them return to a text to find more examples that would support an argument, for example. Often, the students themselves provide a good idea for the next step. Ask them whether the topic is worth pursuing or whether they need to explore it further. You might be surprised how often students come up with an interesting next phase of the assignment on their own.

Finally, consider another arena in which the rules of a discussion may seem as important as the discussion itself: the courtroom. Countless novels and plays hinge on events in the courtroom. The tension is often heightened by the constraints or manipulations of the process. I've found that it doesn't do much good simply to reenact a trial from literature, because such scenes include their own outcome (can you imagine Atticus Finch or John Proctor *winning* their cases?); rather, I find it's interesting to hold trials for characters whose guilt or innocence is ambiguous, but who were never tried in court in the stories in which they appear—Jack from *Lord of the Flies* for the murder of Piggy, or Hamlet, had he lived, for the murder of Polonius. There's a place in such an activity for many students: You might assign roles to a prosecution team, a defense team, a judge, witnesses, jurors, and the accused. The outcome of such a trial is, of course, interesting but not terribly important; it's the fact that students will need to question the text and its themes, to return to the work to gather evidence, and to read carefully that ultimately makes such a lesson both enjoyable and worthwhile.

Connecting to Current Events

A parliamentary simulation such as MUN or Model Congress is used to debate bills or resolutions—documents that enact a law, encourage an action, or provide for a new institution to solve an existing problem. This type of simulation provides its own rewards, and it's easy, I find, to connect the results to literature (rather than starting with literature and then making the connection). In social studies classes, in particular, I might begin with a session of MUN and then assign a work as follow-up reading—or, depending on the subject matter of the course, a simulation of the summit meeting of G-8 nations, the European Congress, the Organization of African Unity, or OPEC.

There is, simply put, no more immediate and relevant activity that I've found for connecting students to current events of a global nature. A discussion in parliamentary form of a UN resolution calling for more aid or military involvement in the Sudan (or, historically, Rwanda) offers deeply important and relevant connections to a study of *Night* or *The Diary of Anne Frank*. A bill calling for a new military draft might produce new insights into *The Things They Carried* or *Catch-22*. Such simulations offer students a multiplicity of ideas and options for exploring a topic; they're an exciting way to elicit more sophisticated and complex thinking about texts and issues that we might otherwise oversimplify.

7 For Further Discussion

This chapter is intended to serve both as a resource and a model. The sample surveys, prompts, quotations, and ideas included here might just offer a ready-made lesson or activity for your own classroom—they've worked for me.

At the same time, I can't possibly provide a discussion survey for every work you might teach, nor can I imagine every prompt a teacher might need at the end of a discussion. Use the activities included here, therefore, also as guides to creating more resources specific to the works you teach, the topics you cover, and the needs of your own classroom. In addition, there are some further guidelines for constructing your own versions of some of the activities in this book.

Here's what's included in this chapter:

- jump-starts and fillers for classroom discussion
- sample discussion surveys
- prompts and statements for discussion activities such as Get Off the Fence, the Fishbowl, and Big Paper discussion
- sample quotations for fast-writing and ending lessons
- a compilation of follow-up ideas from the activities in this book

Jump-Starts and Fillers

Sometimes, a class has trouble getting started on a discussion. In these cases, I use a neutral topic unrelated to our class to get things going, then switch over to a textual question or statement. I also use these to fill time at the end of class—five or ten minutes just for fun. Try them with the discussion techniques outlined in this book.

Here are some model statements (you can easily create more like them).

- Cats are better than dogs.
- The media is too invasive; more laws should be passed to keep the media away from the private lives of celebrities.
- It is better to have two children than to have three.
- America would be a better place if everyone were a vegetarian.
- Artists have to suffer in order to create truly great art.
- There is a good reason why the Harry Potter series was one of the top ten most banned books of the 1990s.
- Every American high school student should have to take at least three years of a foreign language.
- It would be better to have school all year than to have a long summer break.
- High school students should not be allowed to hold jobs during the school year.
- Access to the Internet should be free for every American citizen.
- Seatbelt laws should be abolished.
- Basketball is the greatest sport ever invented by man.
- There should be a time for voluntary silent prayer during every school day in every school.
- Ghosts exist.
- Man will set foot on Mars within the next fifty years.
- Professional athletes in the United States deserve the high salaries they earn.
- The government should redirect all of the money it spends on space exploration toward solutions for domestic problems such as homelessness and poverty.
- Teenagers are generally worse drivers than their parents.

Surveys

Below are nine surveys—six designed to encourage discussion about specific works of literature, three others about current events and issues. Before looking at the surveys themselves, take a look at the short description of each survey that precedes them—a brief statement about what each is designed to measure and what kind of discussion it might elicit. Remember, however, that the overall scale of the survey line is only a springboard toward talking about individual items and, ultimately, individual scenes or issues.

Literature

Although I suggest, for each of the surveys below, the two ends of the spectrum of viewpoints the survey spans, remember that it's a good idea to ask students, first, what they think the opposing viewpoints at either end of the line might be.

The Importance of Being Earnest

This survey, based on Oscar Wilde's play, uses actual scenes from the play and asks students to judge the motivations and thoughts of the characters and of the author himself. The fundamental question this survey attempts to address has to do with how seriously Wilde meant the play to be taken. Is it, after all, a lighthearted and frivolous comedy (as one who scores a fifty might suggest), or is it a scathing commentary on the shallow and bitter nature of the Victorian upper class (a belief indicated by a score of ten)?

Lord of the Flies

The next three surveys draw upon the themes explored within the story of the novels they cover. Any of the statements included might serve as a potential writing prompt for an assignment related to the relevant book. The *Lord of the Flies* survey is fairly straightforward—one who agrees with all of the statements would likely think that Jack's actions are defensible throughout the novel; one who disagrees would support Ralph. One interesting question to ask the students: Where does the character Simon fit on this scale, if he fits at all?

Pride and Prejudice

I've always found teaching Austen to be a challenge: Students either seem to love or hate her work, as do many adults (Mark Twain on this novel: "Every time I read *Pride and Prejudice* I want to dig [Austen] up and beat her over the skull with her own shin-bone"). Eventually, I think, one can only love Austen if one loves her style—the irony, the wit, the syntax—and so I often use group work with a class to encourage such examination of the text as a unit goes on.

To begin the unit, however, I try to give students a sense of the society in which the characters operate, along with its similarities and dissimilarities to our own. It might be tempting for students, after taking this survey, to think that one side represents Mr. Darcy and the other Elizabeth Bennet (or one side "pride" and the other "prejudice"), but it's clear in the novel that Darcy and Elizabeth are not polar opposites. In fact, Elizabeth shares many of the viewpoints of Darcy and society as a whole—just not all of them. Rather, the statements on the survey are designed to reflect the strictest and most conservative beliefs of the society portrayed in the novel and, possibly, of our own. It's also important to note that just as no one character necessarily believes all of these statements to be true, neither does Austen.

A score of ten on this survey, then, indicates radical opposition to the most common values of the society—probably no character in the novel would fit this description, but you might ask students which characters come closest.

Hard Times

This short novel by Dickens serves as an interesting case study for discussions about Victorian society and Victorian literature. As with *Pride and Prejudice,* the survey statements align with beliefs of a conservative element of the society of the novel; a score of fifty indicates agreement with these beliefs, while a score of ten indicates opposition.

The Crucible

Athough the statements on the previous three surveys might serve to connect the themes of those novels with current issues, the survey based on Miller's play, *The Crucible,* is designed specifically to make a connection between the story of the play and the historical context in which it was written. In addition, issues of patriotism, civil liberties, and protest have taken center stage in our national discourse again during the early twenty-first century. The survey makes an interesting springboard for discussions about various political movements: the McCarthy trials of the 1950s, the Patriot Act of recent years, and even issues of protest abroad in comparison to protest at home (one might explore, for instance, the role of the government in protests such as Tiananmen Square, Kent State, or the Civil Rights movement).

A score of fifty generally aligns with a more politically conservative viewpoint of the legitimacy of protest, dissent, and national unity; a score of ten generally aligns with liberal ideas. Applying those labels, however, may be more trouble than it's worth. One might simply attempt to summarize the viewpoints of the extremes of the spectrum, then talk about characters and real historical or political figures and where along the line they might fit.

This is a good opportunity, too, to discuss the fact that characters in fiction and drama are not static—they may grow and learn and thus move along the line. Consider how characters in this play such as John Proctor, his wife Elizabeth, and Reverend Hale adapt their thinking throughout the course of the play.

The Fountainhead

Teaching *The Fountainhead*—a novel I inherited from a previous teacher's summer reading assignments—was a challenge for me. Many students in the AP class that read this book thought it was the best work they'd ever read; suffice it to say I didn't agree. What I didn't want to do was launch into a prolonged criticism of a work whose ideas the students valued, so instead I created this survey, took it along with the class, and placed myself on the line in the appropriate spot to discuss each item.

In this case, every statement on the survey is a direct quotation from the novel, mostly from the dialogue of Howard Roark, Rand's protagonist; thus a score of fifty indicates complete agreement with Roark and, by extension, Rand herself. A few questions you might ask after students take the survey: To what extent does Rand allow viable alternative points of view to be expressed by other characters? How does she manipulate the story to get her message across? What elements of life and society (for example, children, religion) does she leave out entirely?

Current Events and Issues

The Role of the Government

I've seen several surveys that attempt to separate liberals from conservatives on an extremely broad range of social, economic, and international issues such as abortion, homosexual marriage, tax cuts, and war. This survey works along those lines but with a more specific focus; this survey is specifically about the extent to which government should fund certain areas of society and policy. The idea is not simply to offer students a political label but to make them think about how beliefs translate into action or nonaction by the government. Students who score a fifty will generally believe in small government in economic terms, while those at the other end of the scale will believe in more governmental funding. These beliefs often correlate with conservatism in the first case and liberalism in the second, but not necessarily—one might have a high score on this survey and still oppose government involvement in the social arena and issues of morality. One question to ask those students on the low end: Where will the money come from? Similarly, on the high end: What if private citizens simply don't pay for, say, a symphony orchestra or shelters for the homeless?

U.S. Foreign Policy Scenarios

This survey differs from the others in that the scale of one to five does not indicate a degree of agreement but rather a degree of action. Thus, students scoring in the high range will generally support the direct use of force in support of our national interests, with students at the low end generally less inclined to use force and more inclined to seek peaceful resolutions to situations that may involve serious compromises. However, a major caveat is needed: Because the survey uses real-world situations (every item on the survey refers to an actual historical event or general situation), real-world politics apply, as well. Thus, where a student might consider the use of force against a weaker state, he or she might not consider such options viable when dealing with strong militaries. As always, the survey is merely a starting place to reach a discussion of the nuances and intricacies of the topic of foreign policy.

Human Rights Issues

The statements on this survey are paraphrases of various articles of the United Nations Declaration of Human Rights, of which the United States is a signatory. After students take the survey and discuss the items on it (a high score indicates agreement with the document, a low score disagreement), give them the actual document and have them find the relevant articles. The results of this survey are useful for creating small groups (put all of the high scorers together, all of the low scorers together, and so on) for discussions of other international and political issues.

Discussion Survey: *The Importance of Being Earnest*

For each statement below, circle one number:

> 5—*agree strongly*
>
> 4—*agree*
>
> 3—*undecided/equal balance*
>
> 2—*disagree*
>
> 1—*disagree strongly*

1. By the end of the play, it is clear that Algernon and Cecily truly love one another. 5 4 3 2 1

2. By the end of the play, it is clear that Jack (Earnest) and Gwendolyn truly love one another. 5 4 3 2 1

3. It is unlikely that Lady Bracknell would really keep Jack from marrying Gwendolyn forever. 5 4 3 2 1

4. The tension between Jack and Algernon is mostly playful and temporary—underneath it all, they are good friends and respect one another. 5 4 3 2 1

5. Cecily, Gwendolyn, and Lady Bracknell are perfectly content with the position of women in Victorian society. 5 4 3 2 1

6. When Lady Bracknell tells Algernon he should "never speak disrespectfully of Society," she is merely setting up her own follow-up joke: "Only people who can't get into it do that." 5 4 3 2 1

7. Wilde's characters don't seem to learn anything by the end the play because things are funnier that way. 5 4 3 2 1

8. Gwendolyn's remark to Jack at the end of the play—that he is sure to change—is a playful and lighthearted comment on his nature. 5 4 3 2 1

9. At the end of the play, Jack means what he implies—he has learned the importance of being honest. 5 4 3 2 1

10. The play ends happily for everyone. 5 4 3 2 1

Add your score _____

Discussion Survey: *Lord of the Flies*

For each statement below, circle one number:

> 5—*agree strongly*
>
> 4—*agree*
>
> 3—*undecided/equal balance*
>
> 2—*disagree*
>
> 1—*disagree strongly*

1. Human beings are basically selfish.   5 4 3 2 1

2. Arriving at a consensus is less important than getting results.   5 4 3 2 1

3. The leader in any group should not always be the smartest person—it should be the strongest and most decisive person.   5 4 3 2 1

4. Our instincts to hunt and survive are stronger than our instincts to build community.   5 4 3 2 1

5. In many situations, it is better to rely only on your own wits and abilities than to expect someone else to come to your aid.   5 4 3 2 1

6. The human beings who are physically the strongest are most suited to survive in the wilderness.   5 4 3 2 1

7. It is more natural for human beings to form hierarchies than it is for them to work together as equals.   5 4 3 2 1

8. Every human being should ensure his or her own survival before making a sacrifice to ensure another's survival.   5 4 3 2 1

9. There is no reason for a human being not to eat meat.   5 4 3 2 1

10. Fear is the most useful tool for controling a group.   5 4 3 2 1

Add your score   _____

Discussion Survey: *Pride and Prejudice*

For each statement below, circle one number:

> *5—agree strongly*
>
> *4—agree*
>
> *3—undecided/equal balance*
>
> *2—disagree*
>
> *1—disagree strongly*

1. It is better to marry within one's own social class than outside 5 4 3 2 1
   of it.

2. The most important decision a woman makes in her life is the 5 4 3 2 1
   decision of whom to marry.

3. A person's moral values, judgment, and quality of character 5 4 3 2 1
   are reflected by and can be measured by the qualities of his or
   her family.

4. It is generally better to follow the expectations of society than 5 4 3 2 1
   one's own desires and emotional whims.

5. When choosing a spouse, one should consider financial issues 5 4 3 2 1
   and social security as well as love.

6. It is better to seem arrogant than it is to lower one's standards 5 4 3 2 1
   or compromise one's character.

7. There are truths that should be universally acknowledged. 5 4 3 2 1

8. A successful relationship requires the consent of one's parents, 5 4 3 2 1
   guardians, or elder relatives.

9. The purpose of a woman's education is to make her a more 5 4 3 2 1
   attractive prospect for marriage.

10. One should not get married before one's older siblings. 5 4 3 2 1

Add your score _____

Discussion Survey: *Hard Times*

For each statement below, circle one number:

> 5—*agree strongly*
>
> 4—*agree*
>
> 3—*undecided/equal balance*
>
> 2—*disagree*
>
> 1—*disagree strongly*

1. When faced with a decision, it is more important to know the facts of a situation than to use imagination in determining possible outcomes. 5 4 3 2 1

2. In a capitalist society, most people who are poor just don't work hard enough or aren't smart enough to succeed. 5 4 3 2 1

3. Art has its place, but science is more important for humanity in the long run. 5 4 3 2 1

4. Progress for mankind is more important than concerns about the environment. 5 4 3 2 1

5. People of different social classes or degrees of wealth will rarely be able to sustain a romantic relationship. 5 4 3 2 1

6. Our education system should include time for the arts, creative writing, and activities, but should spend more time teaching basic skills in math, science, and grammar. 5 4 3 2 1

7. People usually get what they deserve. 5 4 3 2 1

8. The best way of protesting social injustice is to study and pass laws; this is more effective than writing novels or making movies. 5 4 3 2 1

9. Because our economic system is based on self-interest, the poor will remain poor and the rich will remain rich. 5 4 3 2 1

10. The society Dickens portrays in *Hard Times* bears little resemblance to our society today. 5 4 3 2 1

Add your score _____

Discussion Survey: Issues from *The Crucible*

For each statement below, circle one number:

> 5—*agree strongly*
>
> 4—*agree*
>
> 3—*undecided/equal balance*
>
> 2—*disagree*
>
> 1—*disagree strongly*

1. The good of society is more important than the rights of any one citizen. 5 4 3 2 1

2. It is possible for American citizens to express opinions that are un-American. 5 4 3 2 1

3. Sometimes protest against American policies is dangerous and should be prohibited. 5 4 3 2 1

4. The greatest threat to the United States during the twentieth century was Communism. 5 4 3 2 1

5. It is not possible to be partly against or for America; one is either pro-American or anti-American. 5 4 3 2 1

6. Strength comes from unity; a society that accepts many opinions and beliefs is always weaker than one that does not. 5 4 3 2 1

7. Political beliefs can be dangerous and therefore public officials should have the right to question citizens about their beliefs. 5 4 3 2 1

8. People can be guilty by association; if you associate with criminals, you too are a criminal. 5 4 3 2 1

9. It is important that those who act against the interests of America are punished publicly so that their punishment acts as an example to others. 5 4 3 2 1

10. Those who commit moral sins are likely to commit legal crimes as well. 5 4 3 2 1

Add your score _____

Discussion Survey: Quotations from *The Fountainhead*

For each statement below, circle one number:

> *5—agree strongly*
>
> *4—agree*
>
> *3—undecided/equal balance*
>
> *2—disagree*
>
> *1—disagree strongly*

1. The man who attempts to live for others is a parasite in motive and makes parasites of those he serves.　　5　4　3　2　1

2. There is no such thing as a collective thought.　　5　4　3　2　1

3. No work is ever done collectively, by a majority decision. Every creative job is achieved under the guidance of a single individual thought.　　5　4　3　2　1

4. Man's moral obligation is to do what he wishes, provided his wish does not depend *primarily* upon other men.　　5　4　3　2　1

5. The integrity of a man's creative work is of greater importance than any charitable endeavor.　　5　4　3　2　1

6. Every major horror in history was committed in the name of an altruistic motive.　　5　4　3　2　1

7. Man cannot survive except through his mind. He comes on earth unarmed. His brain is his only weapon.　　5　4　3　2　1

8. America's abundance was not created by public sacrifices to the common good, but by the productive genius of free men who pursued their own personal interests and the making of their own private fortunes.　　5　4　3　2　1

9. Neither life nor happiness can be achieved by the pursuit of irrational whims.　　5　4　3　2　1

10. Man must live for his own sake, neither sacrificing himself to others nor sacrificing others to himself.　　5　4　3　2　1

Add your score _____

Discussion Survey – The Role of the Government

Which of the following is most responsible for funding each of the following areas?

5—*Funding is entirely the responsibility of private citizens.*

4—*Funding is mostly the responsibility of private citizens.*

3—*Private citizens and the government should share costs equally.*

2—*Funding is mostly the responsibility of the government.*

1—*Funding is entirely the responsibility of the government.*

1. shelters and programs for the homeless   5   4   3   2   1

2. child care for poor working parents   5   4   3   2   1

3. the preservation of parks and other natural resources   5   4   3   2   1

4. major artistic endeavors such as symphony orchestras, theater   5   4   3   2   1
    and dance companies, and art museums

5. arts education and instruction in schools   5   4   3   2   1

6. programs and resources to educate students about AIDS and   5   4   3   2   1
    other diseases

7. construction of professional sports arenas   5   4   3   2   1

8. curbside recycling programs   5   4   3   2   1

9. health care for poor senior citizens   5   4   3   2   1

10. legal fees for death row inmates' appeals   5   4   3   2   1

Add your score _____

Discussion Survey: U.S. Foreign Policy Scenarios

For each scenario below, circle the number of the most appropriate U.S. response:

5—military action

4—military threat

3—sanctions, embargo, or formal protest

2—bilateral/multilateral negotiations

1—nonaction or appeasement

1. North Korea continues its efforts to build a nuclear weapons program.   5 4 3 2 1

2. A shari'a court in northern Nigeria sentences a woman to be stoned for committing adultery.   5 4 3 2 1

3. Reports of widespread human rights abuses in China continue.   5 4 3 2 1

4. Israel assassinates a man it claims to be the leader of Hamas, killing several civilians in the process.   5 4 3 2 1

5. A U.S. military plane crashes in China during an un-authorized flight into Chinese airspace—the plane carries valuable military secrets and China refuses to return it to the United States.   5 4 3 2 1

6. Suspicions are voiced that Iran has purchased components for the production of nuclear weapons.   5 4 3 2 1

7. China conducts military tests off the coast of Taiwan.   5 4 3 2 1

8. One African nation dams water, leaving thousands in a smaller nation downriver without water and dying.   5 4 3 2 1

9. After terrorists take over a Russian building, the Russian government gasses the building, killing the terrorists and hundreds of hostages.   5 4 3 2 1

10. While the United States is building trade relations with another nation, U.S. citizens in that nation are taken hostage by rogue terrorist groups.   5 4 3 2 1

Add your score   _____

Discussion Survey: Human Rights

For each statement below, circle one number:

   5—*agree strongly*

   4—*agree*

   3—*undecided/equal balance*

   2—*disagree*

   1—*disagree strongly*

All human beings have the right:

1. not to be tortured for any reason   5   4   3   2   1

2. to leave and return to their countries   5   4   3   2   1

3. to marry and found a family   5   4   3   2   1

4. to practice any religion they wish   5   4   3   2   1

5. to vote   5   4   3   2   1

6. to have access to a government-sponsored social security   5   4   3   2   1
    program

7. to join a trade union   5   4   3   2   1

8. to have periodic holidays with pay   5   4   3   2   1

9. to free education as a child   5   4   3   2   1

10. to make money from their own artistic or scientific creations   5   4   3   2   1

Add your score   _____

Discussion Prompts for Get Off the Fence, Fishbowl, and Big Paper Discussions

The following lists of statements are useful for sparking discussion either with the whole class or in groups and pairs. The statements are intentionally provocative and one-sided. The point of discussion, of course, is not just to state agreement or disagreement with the statement but to explore the nuances of the issue. It's always a good idea to think through not just the most obvious alternative to the statement—the opposite point of view—but also to question parts of the statement and consider stances that include only partial agreement; as a discussion facilitator, I consider it my role to provide such arguments when they're not being raised by the class (regardless of my personal beliefs).

Literature

General Prompts About Literature

These statements are phrased in general terms but can easily be modified to refer to a single work.

- No work of literary merit can have a completely happy ending.
- No male author can create a convincing female character (or vice versa).
- Authors don't consciously put symbols into a work—they just write stories and then English teachers impose meaning on objects and call them symbolic.
- Ultimately, the best indicator of good literature is that it entertains the reader.
- Villains are almost always more interesting to read about than heroes.
- The opening sentence of a novel or play is the most important one.
- Every good work of literature is, at its heart, either a mystery story, a travel journal, or a story about falling in love.
- All literary characters can be divided into three categories: hero, victim, or fool.
- A character can do the right thing for the right reasons, the wrong thing for the right reasons, or the wrong thing for the wrong reasons—but it's not possible for a character to do the right thing for the wrong reasons.

- It's better to know the biography of an author before reading his or her books than simply to read the book out of context.
- A poem that does not rhyme is not a poem.
- The greatest novels are unclassifiable—they do not fall into any particular genre and have no particular audience other than readers.
- The twentieth century will not be remembered for its books.

Tragic Literature

- To be a tragedy, a work must have a tragic hero.
- To be a tragic hero, a character must have a tragic flaw.
- No novel is a true tragedy—at best, a novel might be a dramatic story with a tragic situation.
- A tragedy must be about important or upper-class figures in society for the outcome to have the greatest impact on the audience—the common person is never a tragic figure.
- There are no great female tragic heroes.
- For the audience to feel tragedy deeply, the story must involve a romantic relationship, even if that relationship is secondary to the main plot.
- A tragic hero can only exist when the mechanisms of the state are working against him or her in some way.
- Every tragic story could also be written as a comedy.
- Tragic works of literature, when successful, make us feel better because they leave us with a heightened sense of right and wrong.

Middle School Fantasy Literature (Harry Potter and the Sorcerer's Stone, The Once and Future King, Eragon, A Wrinkle in Time, The Lord of the Rings, *and so on*)

Although I classify the above works as middle school literature, in fact, such novels engage (and sometimes challenge) high school readers, as well. I never discourage such reading—a student who loves to read the Harry Potter books is, after all, reading—but I do encourage students to read with at least some critical awareness. The following prompts not only guide students in their exploration of the themes of these fantasy works but are also useful means for comparing such works to other literature. The trick here, I find, is not to be too judgmental nor too enthusiastic about genre literature but rather to help students become thoughtful consumers of the works they enjoy without diminishing that enjoyment.

- Only by embarking on a physical journey can one explore one's own feelings and abilities.

- Every great story involves a search for one's parents, one's origins, and one's identity.

- Only in books and stories does true evil exist—but even in books and stories there are often shades and degrees of villainy.

- Even when true evil exists and is identifiable in a story, it is the human characters who oppose the protagonist whom we most detest.

- Literature can either be realistic or it can entertain—it cannot do both.

- A story in which the side of good wins entirely is rarely as satisfying or as true to life as a story in which good prevails conditionally.

- In fantasy literature, the sequel is always more enjoyable than the first book.

- Every great hero has a great mentor, guide, or teacher.

- Fantasy literature is for boys.

- Books that depict witchcraft in a favorable light also encourage witchcraft and should, therefore, not be taught in schools.

And my personal favorite:

- The best fantasy story ever written would contain a ghost, a murder, a hero's search for his parents and identity, a pirate ship, a great swordfight, romance, and an evil, villainous king—in short, it would be *Hamlet*.

Current Events and Issues

Education

- All students in U.S. public schools should be taught only in English.

- It is important for public schools to teach moral values.

- It is important for public schools to teach Christian values.

- The safety of an entire school is more important that the rights of any one student.

- No student who cannot read at a tenth-grade level should graduate from high school.

- Teachers should have to pass a competency test in their subject areas every five years.

- Students who cheat on tests should be suspended after the first offense.
- Students who see others cheat and do not turn them in should be punished.
- The only way in which a teacher should teach "sex education" in public schools is by encouraging abstinence.
- Parents should be allowed to use money spent by the government on the education of their children to pay for private school tuition.
- "Tracking" (assigning students to classes based on their previous academic performance) is inherently unfair and should not be allowed in public schools—all courses should be open to all students.
- Schools should be open on Martin Luther King Jr. Day.
- Students should not be excused for religious holidays other than those on which the entire school is closed.
- Student uniforms should be required in all schools.
- School administrators should review and, when needed, edit school publications to reflect the values and beliefs of the school community.

Overpopulation

The world population has been growing rapidly for the past several decades. Although there is debate among experts about whether or not population is exploding or gradually stabilizing, there is no doubt that in some countries, population growth continues at an extremely rapid rate. The following statements are useful prompts for a discussion of overpopulation, but it's worthwhile to have students do some research first—have them, for instance, look up estimates of world population growth over the next fifty years, population growth figures for the past fifty years, nations with the largest population growth, and facts about attempts to slow population growth (especially in China and India).

- Governments have a responsibility to slow population growth within their own borders, even at the expense of individual liberties and rights.
- India and Nigeria should adopt family planning laws modeled after those in China.
- Nations with high population growth rates should divert all available resources toward education, literacy programs, and putting women to work.

- Social security programs are necessary in order to ensure that the extremely poor do not continue to have more children than they can support.

- Nations in which population growth is a problem should increase the use of the death penalty dramatically.

- Rather than promoting birth control through the distribution of condoms and other devices, governments should promote abstinence.

- Any efforts at curbing population growth must be directed at the women of a nation, not the men.

- In societies where overpopulation is a problem, those who have more children than they can support are entirely to blame for the problem and should be left to deal with it themselves.

- No matter how many problems overpopulation causes in a nation, small minority groups should be encouraged to have more children.

Citizenship and Governance

The following prompts work well as starters for discussions about literature, as well.

- Citizens who protest against a government or its laws usually end up doing more harm than good.

- It is very often the case that those with a great deal of wealth are most suited to serve as legislators and leaders.

- When a government declares war, every citizen in the nation should support that war.

- Government exists to protect the rights of society's weakest members, not the rights of the majority.

- Governments have the responsibility to legislate morality.

- Diversity creates weaker and less stable societies and governments.

- There is a place for religion in government.

- Democracy is not the best alternative for every country—some societies need authoritarian rule to survive.

- A smart, strong leader is the most valuable asset a nation can have.

- Minority groups, whether they be formed by gender, ethnicity, or culture, are responsible for elevating their own status—and should shoulder the most blame when they do not do so.

- The identity of a society is shaped by its conflicts.

Current Events and Issues (United States)

- The U.S. Constitution should be amended to make burning an American flag a criminal act.
- Every U.S. citizen should be required to spend two years serving the government in the military or some form of civil service.
- All U.S. college admissions should be blind—no weight should be given to race, gender, or other physical characteristics in the selection of students.
- Every child in the United States should be taught how to operate a handgun safely.
- Feminism is unnecessary.
- The United States should strengthen its immigration law and allow far fewer immigrants to enter this country legally.
- Children of illegal immigrants should not be allowed to attend schools or receive health care at hospitals.
- Smoking should be illegal in all restaurants in the United States.
- If it saves the government money, federal prisons should be owned and operated by private companies.
- Capital punishment is a human rights abuse.
- All laws about marriage should be made at the state, not the federal, level.
- Whether the government endorses racial profiling as a policy or not, racial profiling is constantly used by police and government agencies.

Current Events and Issues (International)

- The best hope for world peace in the future rests in a strong and unified United Nations.
- The right to develop and own nuclear weapons is a sovereign right of every nation.
- Less-developed nations must develop on their own—no amount of aid from Western developed nations will ultimately strengthen the societies of these countries.
- It is less important for Americans to learn a foreign language than it is for citizens of other nations to learn to speak English.
- The only guarantee of peace between two nations is equality of military strength.
- We should strive to make all nations democratic.

- The majority of wars in the future will not be international wars, but conflicts within nations.

- The worst threat facing the world is not terrorism or traditional warfare but overpopulation and disease.

- All acts of terrorism are essentially acts of cowardice.

- Nations can be good or evil.

- Right and wrong are not values that are relative or dependent on culture.

- The best way to stop human rights abuses is to place sanctions on those countries who abuse human rights.

- The only effective means of combating poverty, disease, and hunger around the world is education.

Sample Quotations for Fast-Writing and Concluding Discussions

The most interesting discussions are not always the most satisfying to students, as good discussions often raise unanswered or complicated questions. In order to provide some sense of closure, I like to offer students a last chance to reflect on the topic of the discussion—to talk about a specific quotation for the final few minutes of a class period, to summarize their thoughts by responding to a specific statement or idea, or just to continue the process of thinking about the topic at hand. The following quotations include statements that are useful for concluding discussions about literature and about current events and issues.

Reading

"Every reader is, when he reads, reading only about himself."
—Marcel Proust

"Imaginative readers rewrite books to suit their own taste, omitting and mentally altering what they read."
—Robert Graves

"It is absurd to have a hard and fast rule about what one should read and what one shouldn't."
—Oscar Wilde

"There are three kinds of readers: one, who enjoys without judging; a third, who judges without enjoying; another in the middle, who judges while enjoying and enjoys while judging."
—Johann Wolfgang von Goethe

"Words are undervalued as a means of expression. Pictures tend to trivialize experience."

—Arthur Miller

"The only books that influence us are those for which we are ready."

—E. M. Forster

"Dictators are as scared of books as they are of the cannon."

—Harry Golden

"Poetry is a way of taking life by the throat."

—Robert Frost

"Genuine poetry can communicate before it is understood."

—T. S. Eliot

"Literature is a luxury; fiction is a necessity."

—G. K. Chesterton

Writing

"Writers, like teeth, are divided into incisors and grinders."

—Walter Bagehot

"One of the things a writer is for is to say the unsayable, speak the unspeakable and ask difficult questions."

—Salman Rushdie

"The only end of writing is to enable the readers better to enjoy life, or better to endure it."

—Samuel Johnson

"An author ought to write for the youth of his own generation, the critics of the next, and the schoolmasters of ever after."

—F. Scott Fitzgerald

"A pen, as well as a silver bullet, can draw blood."

—Graham Greene

"Poetry makes things happen, but rarely what the poet wants."

—Howard Nemerov

"Writing a novel is actually searching for victims. As I write I keep looking for casualties."

—John Irving

"No one in his right mind would sit down to write a book if he were a well-adjusted, happy man."

—Jay McInerney

Education and Learning

"An education isn't how much you have committed to memory, or even how much you know. It's being able to differentiate between what you do know and what you don't."

—Anatole France

"The foundation of every state is the education of its youth."

—Diogenes Laertius

"America believes in education: the average professor earns more money in a year than a professional athlete earns in a whole week."

—Evan Esar

"Next in importance to freedom and justice is popular education, without which neither freedom nor justice can be permanently maintained."

—James A. Garfield

"I respect faith, but doubt is what gets you an education."

—Wilson Mizner

American Society

"America is a large, friendly dog in a very small room. Every time it wags its tail, it knocks over a chair."

—Arnold Toynbee

"The United States is a nation of laws: badly written and randomly enforced."

—Frank Zappa

"It is, I think, an indisputable fact that Americans are, as Americans, the most self-conscious people in the world, and the most addicted to the belief that the other nations are in a conspiracy to under-value them."

—Henry James

"The American, by nature, is optimistic. He is experimental, an inventor and a builder who builds best when called upon to build greatly."

—John F. Kennedy

"A citizen of America will cross the ocean to fight for democracy, but won't cross the street to vote in a national election."

—Bill Vaughan

Governance and Freedom

"A nation is a society united by delusions about its ancestry and by common hatred of its neighbors."

—William Ralph Inge

"My definition of a free society is a society where it is safe to be unpopular."

—Adlai E. Stevenson Jr.

"In the truest sense, freedom cannot be bestowed; it must be achieved."

—Franklin D. Roosevelt

"While the State exists, there can be no freedom. When there is freedom there will be no State."

—Vladimir Lenin

"Most of the change we think we see in life is due to truths being in and out of favor."

—Robert Frost

"It is dangerous to be right when the government is wrong."

—Voltaire

"I like to believe that people in the long run are going to do more to promote peace than our governments. Indeed, I think that people want peace so much that one of these days governments had better get out of the way and let them have it."

—Dwight D. Eisenhower

"Every decent man is ashamed of the government he lives under."

—H. L. Mencken

"No government can be long secure without formidable opposition."

—Benjamin Disraeli

"Since love and fear can hardly exist together, if we must choose between them, it is far safer to be feared than loved."

—Niccolo Machiavelli

War and Conflict

Note: Although several of the following quotations refer to individuals, it can be interesting to discuss with students whether or not they're true if applied to cultures and nations.

> "War is not nice."
>
> —Barbara Bush

> "Victorious warriors win first and then go to war, while defeated warriors go to war first and then seek to win."
>
> —Sun-Tzu

> "No one can guarantee success in war, but only deserve it."
>
> —Winston Churchill

> "Among other evils which being unarmed brings you, it causes you to be despised."
>
> —Niccolo Machiavelli

> "All's fair in love and war."
>
> —Francis Edward Smedley

> "To be prepared for war is one of the most effective means of preserving peace."
>
> —George Washington

> "As long as there are sovereign nations possessing great power, war is inevitable."
>
> —Albert Einstein

A Compilation of Follow-up Ideas

After a discussion, instruct your students to complete the following activities during the remainder of a class period, as homework, or as an assignment during a subsequent class.

- Write about the topic or in response to a follow-up idea, quotation, or passage (fast-writing, essay, creative writing).
- Return to the text to look for examples that illustrate the idea or issue.
- Research to find out what others think about the issue—return with quotations, facts, or articles that address the topic.

- Reflect on current events by checking news stories and articles.
- Compare or contrast the treatment of an issue in one text with the treatment in other works you've studied.
- Reflect on the discussion itself—summarize viewpoints of class members and state your own position on the issue.
- Compare the product of the activity or discussion to a product from earlier in the year, from a previous class, or from another section of the course.
- Use the product of an activity to "teach" one another—lead a discussion, give a presentation, or work in groups.
- Further organize ideas gathered in an activity—come up with more ways of examining and understanding the material that has come up in class.
- Work on the product of an activity for classroom display.
- Look over the written product of a discussion or class activity, isolate parts of the product that could be explored in greater depth and detail, and then work on a new product using those details (layering).
- Hold an online chat or email discussion about the topic or a follow-up topic with others in the class.
- Broaden the audience of student discussions by having them discuss online with students in other class periods or even other schools.
- Create a rubric that will be used to score your own work and conduct self-assessment.
- Create displays and files using digital recording and photography to share with other students, administrators, or even parents.
- Reflect on a topic or story by writing a separate defense of each side or position.
- Write a letter to the editor taking a stance on an important issue.
- Compare a class product to an actual historical document or other text.

Appendix: Useful Information

A Note About Standards

I don't know how most teachers think, but I suspect that a number of them think about standards the way I do—after the fact. State and national standards don't seem inherently harmful to me, but neither do they really guide the way I teach; rather, when I'm asked to discuss how my teaching reflects the standards, I tend to think of the activities that work first and the overall standards that encompass those activities almost as an afterthought.

At their best, of course, that's what standards should do—identify what great teachers do correctly by instinct and serve as guides, but not straitjackets, for all of us. I find that the national standards published by the National Council of Teachers of English and the International Reading Association (there are twelve of them) serve as a good exemplar; not only are the twelve standards on this list reasonable and general, they are published with the idea that the purpose is not to restrict what teachers do but to help identify what our goals should be. As the introduction to the standards (you can find them easily with a Google search or at the websites of the organizations mentioned above) states, "The vision guiding these standards is that all students must have the opportunities and resources to develop the language skills they need to pursue life's goals and to participate fully as informed, productive members of society." What could be more in tune with the purpose of most English (and Social Studies) teachers than that? What do we want if not to give our students life skills?

Although state standards (and other independently formed standards, such as those my school uses) might vary in detail and scope, they generally cover the same basic territory as these national standards and as each other. Here, then, are some general areas of English and Language Arts pedagogy that recur frequently in lists of standards. Note that these particular statements don't correspond specifically to any published list of standards—they are my own paraphrase of common standards for English teachers.

Students should be able to:

1. comprehend and analyze texts of all types—print and non-print, fiction and nonfiction, oral and written, all genres
2. make personal connections to texts and language
3. make connections between texts and thematic areas
4. communicate in written language effectively
5. communicate in spoken language effectively
6. conduct research effectively
7. use information technologies
8. understand and appreciate diverse uses of language—vocabularies, dialects, and modes of discourse
9. apply their understanding of language structures, patterns, and style
10. use language for a variety of purposes—persuasion, analysis, creative expression, and so on
11. adjust their own style of communication (oral and written) to fit different audiences

Let's stipulate, shall we, that every exercise in this book is designed to help students attain the first three of these goals? These standards are generally near the top of every list. They may be subdivided or rephrased, but they're always there because they're the primary goal of any discussion or analytical activity—to understand language and learn from it about yourself and the world, as well as to understand the body of literature as a whole.

That leaves eight standards on my list. Here, then, is a list of the activities in presented in Chapters 2 through 6 of this book, with the numbers of the standards above that apply to aspects of each:

- Survey Lines (5, 11)
- Get Off the Fence (5, 6)
- The Grid (5, 6)
- The Fishbowl (4, 5)
- Brainstorming Groups (5, 9)

- Idea Pass-Arounds (4, 5)
- Wall Posters (4, 5, 11)
- Combining Voices (4, 5, 10, 11)
- Silent Discussion (4, 10)
- The Electronic Conversation (4, 7, 8, 10, 11)
- In the Forum (4, 7, 8, 10, 11)
- Tracking Changes (4, 7, 9, 10)
- A Thousand Words (4, 5, 7, 10)
- Debate (5, 6, 9, 10, 11)
- Rules of Order (4, 5, 6, 9, 10, 11)

Works Mentioned in this Book

The list below includes every novel or play mentioned in this book, along with the sections in which each work is mentioned. Some of the works are mentioned only in passing; others serve as the main focus of a sample lesson.

1984	The Fishbowl, Wall Posters, Debate
A Comedy of Errors	In the Forum
A Man for All Seasons	The Grid, Combining Voices
A Midsummer Night's Dream	The Fishbowl, Combining Voices
A Portrait of the Artist as a Young Man	Combining Voices
A Tale of Two Cities	The Electronic Conversation, In the Forum
Ali and Nino	Combining Voices
All Quiet on the Western Front	Combining Voices
All's Well That Ends Well	In the Forum
Animal Farm	The Fishbowl
Antigone	The Grid, Debate
The Beach	Wall Posters
Beowulf	The Fishbowl
Brave New World	The Fishbowl, Wall Posters
The Canterbury Tales	Combining Voices, Rules of Order
Catch-22	Combining Voices, Rules of Order
The Crucible	The Grid, Combining Voices, For Further Discussion
The Diary of Anne Frank	Rules of Order
Death of a Salesman	The Fishbowl
The Dispossessed	Wall Posters
Erewhon	Wall Posters
The Fountainhead	For Further Discussion
The Giver	Wall Posters

The God of Small Things	In the Forum
The Grapes of Wrath	The Fishbowl, Idea Pass-Arounds, Wall Posters, Combining Voices
The Great Gatsby	The Fishbowl
Grendel	In the Forum
Hamlet	The Grid, Wall Posters
Hard Times	For Further Discussion
Herland	Wall Posters
The House on Mango Street	The Fishbowl, Brainstorming Groups, Combining Voices, Silent Discussion
Howard's End	Silent Discussion
The Importance of Being Earnest	For Further Discussion
Inherit the Wind	The Grid
Invisible Man	The Fishbowl, Combining Voices
Island	Wall Posters
Lord of the Flies	The Grid, The Fishbowl, Wall Posters, Rules of Order, For Further Discussion
The Merchant of Venice	The Fishbowl
Morality Play	Tracking Changes
Night	Rules of Order
Of Mice and Men	The Fishbowl
One Flew over the Cuckoo's Nest	Combining Voices
Othello	Silent Discussion, In the Forum
Paradise Lost	Wall Posters
Peace Like a River	Combining Voices
The Piano Tuner	In the Forum
Poetics	Rules of Order
The Poisonwood Bible	Brainstorming Groups, Combining Voices

Pride and Prejudice	Brainstorming Groups, Combining Voices, For Further Discussion
R&G Are Dead	In the Forum
Romeo and Juliet	Surveys, Combining Voices
Sacred Hunger	Wall Posters
The Shipping News	The Fishbowl
A Streetcar Named Desire	Rules of Order
The Tempest	Wall Posters
The Things They Carried	The Fishbowl, Combining Voices, Rules of Order
To Kill a Mockingbird	The Fishbowl, Wall Posters
The Tortilla Curtain	Combining Voices
The Unvanquished	Get Off the Fence
We	Wall Posters